Richard Layard is one of th
thinkers influencing the Labour
LSE's Centre for Economic Performance, the leading economic research centre in Europe, and is well known for his work on skills and jobs. He is a member of the IPPR's Commission on Public Policy and British Business, which was set up with encouragement from Tony Blair and issued its report in January 1997. Richard Layard also writes regularly for the *Financial Times* and is a frequent contributor to BBC television and radio. In 1985 he founded the Employment Policy Institute, which campaigns against unemployment.

WHAT LABOUR CAN DO

Richard Layard

WARNER BOOKS

A *Warner* Book

First published in Great Britain in 1997
by Warner Books

Text copyright © 1997 by Richard Layard
Illustrations copyright © 1997 by Bobby Hunt

The moral right of the author has been asserted.

All rights reserved.
No part of this publication may be reproduced,
stored in a retrieval system, or transmitted,
in any form or by any means, without the prior
permission in writing of the publisher, nor be
otherwise circulated in any form of binding or cover
other than that in which it is published and without
a similar condition including this condition being
imposed on the subsequent purchaser.

A CIP catalogue record for this book
is available from the British Library.

ISBN: 0 7515 1975 8

Typeset by M Rules in Plantin
Printed and bound in Great Britain
by Clays Ltd, St Ives plc

Warner Books
A Division of
Little, Brown & Company (UK)
Brettenham House
Lancaster Place
London WC2E 7EN

Contents

Introduction vii
Preface xi

1 *Which Way Britain?* 3
2 *The Keys to Success* 11
3 *A Skills Revolution* 29
4 *From Welfare to Work* 55
5 *The Proper Size of Government* 81
6 *Long-term Growth – Not Short-term Profit* 101
7 *No More Boom and Bust* 121
8 *Joining Europe's Currency* 133
9 *Can Labour Do It?* 149

Notes 155
Labour Party Policy Documents 177
References 179
Index 195

Introduction

I WAS BROUGHT UP in the 1950s and '60s to believe in Britain as a society where, even while there was inequality of income and wealth, there was equality of opportunity. For most British people, that belief in equality of opportunity was a central tenet – and still is.

But in Britain today we do not have equality of opportunity. In 1979, one child in eight was brought up in poverty. Today it is one child in three. In 1979, 8 per cent of families had no one in their households earning a wage. Nobody could seriously contend that in Britain today there is equality of opportunity, when almost 20 per cent of families have no wage-earner in the household.

This denial of opportunity offends our basic concept of fair play. And it affects all of us because, whether it is in high social-security bills and high taxes, or in the waste of economic potential, every one of us pays a heavy price as a result. But, most of all, it damages our economy.

In the industrial age, the denial of opportunity – social, economic and political – offended many people but it was not critical to the success of the economy. In this, the information age, it has also become an unacceptable inefficiency, a barrier to prosperity. We are moving from an old industrial economy, one based on mass production in purely national capital markets, to an information- and knowledge-based economy – an economy characterised by global markets, instantaneous communications and new, technology-driven, custom-built products.

And what makes today's society qualitatively different is, first of all, the extent, speed and all-pervasiveness of change which requires companies and people who are flexible and adaptable. Secondly, when raw materials, capital and inventions can be acquired from just about anywhere, what makes the difference to the success or failure of a company, indeed a nation, lies in the potential, the skills and talent of its people.

The twenty-first-century workplace will transform our lives. Women will soon form the majority of the workforce. The old commonplaces – the 40-hour week, the 48-week year, the 48-year working life – are already going. There will be no jobs for life but, at best, a career encompassing many jobs.

Is Britain prepared for this new economy? In Britain today, 33% – one third – of adults have no qualification of any sort to their name; 40% of 21-year-olds report difficulty writing and spelling, let alone computer literacy; and 70% have no education beyond school. But in the new twenty-first-century economy, everyone will need to continue in education or training in some form after school, every teenager must have a skill or qualification, and everyone should have the chance of lifelong learning.

In this modern economy, no job will last a lifetime and no qualification will last a lifetime. So no disadvantage should last a lifetime either; no missed opportunity should last a lifetime, no potential should remain undeveloped for a lifetime. And the task of government is to help people to bridge the gap between what they are and what they have in themselves to become.

Introduction

In place of the old style, one-off equality of opportunity – the one-strike-and-you're-out opportunity – we need lifetime, recurrent, permanent opportunities: second, third, fourth and fifth chances which open up the prospect of opportunities at any age, at any place, at any time and for any study. And it is the mutually reinforcing concept of education and employment opportunity together that offers opportunity to individuals throughout their lives.

Labour's policies – our New Deal for the young and long-term unemployed; our University for Industry; the new constitutional settlement; higher standards in our schools; nursery education for all; a public–private partnership for renovating our social and economic fabric; the new Individual Learning Accounts for all those over sixteen – all flow from and reflect these values.

Richard Layard's book presents his own views, not those of the Labour Party. But he also understands the huge and revolutionary changes that the global economy brings, and the danger of Britain falling further behind if we do not equip our people and companies for the future. And he, more than most, knows that we live in a very different labour market, one which demands greater flexibility from individuals but also active government to provide new employment opportunities for all.

This book is an important contribution to the economic armoury of progressive British politics. It is a clarion call for change, and maps out a challenging reform agenda which any incoming government must consider seriously.

Gordon Brown MP
Shadow Chancellor

Preface

WOULD A LABOUR victory in the general election make a difference to our lives? I believe it would. There is a lot that Labour can do. In this book I set out the main economic measures that could be taken. Some are Labour policy, others are not. The book reflects my views alone and implies nothing about current or future Labour policy. So this is not a Labour Party book. But I hope it can clarify the policy debate and help voters to decide what they think is possible.

In thinking about these issues over the years, I have benefited enormously from the work of my colleagues in the LSE's Centre for Economic Performance. The Centre covers the whole range of issues discussed in this book, and its comradely spirit of intellectual enquiry exemplifies, I like to think, some of the principles advocated in the book. Much of the Centre's work is presented in popular form in its journal *Centrepiece*.[1]

I have also learned a great deal from my distinguished colleagues on the Commission on Public Policy and British Business, whose report was published in January 1997.[2]

While writing the book, I have received generous help and comments from E. Balls, M. Barber, C. Bean, W. Buiter, A. Dilnot, M. Emerson, R. Freeman, P. Gregg, J. Hills, R. Jackman, P. Johnson, D. Leader, C. Mayer, D. Metcalf, S. Nickell, A. Oswald, G. Owen, D. Piauchaud, W. Robinson, and H. Steedman. Tim Hughes provided excellent research assistance, followed by Fernando Goni. The script was superbly typed by Philomena McNicholas.

Needless to say, one's views on the detail of policy develop as evidence and arguments accumulate, but I would be surprised if I were to change my views on the basic principles.

I am grateful to Richard Lambert for suggesting I write the book and to Andrew Gordon, Alan Samson and Michael Shaw for encouragement and help with its publication. I hope the reader will find it useful.

Richard Layard
London, December 1996

WHAT LABOUR CAN DO

1

Which Way Britain?

People, not walls, make a city.
Thucydides

AFTER EIGHTEEN YEARS, has Thatcherism given us what we wanted? Or is there another way, which would make Britain a better place to live for more of its people? That is the issue now facing Britain. What, realistically, could Labour do to improve our lives? The aim of this book is to provide answers, based on solid evidence.[1]

THE PROBLEM

In many ways we live in a wonderful country, and much has improved in the last twenty years. Most people are richer, even in the public sector. Management is more dynamic, and customers are treated better.

But, at the same time, a great deal is wrong. The economy is not working as it should. Britain is still poorer than the rest of Northern Europe, and it is not catching up. The rich have done very well, but the poor have made little progress. Britain is now a more unequal society than any advanced country except the United States. Even those earning good money feel more insecure, after living through two of Europe's largest post-war recessions. Unemployment and crime have soared – and family break-up is on the increase. The workplace is increasingly a rat-race: colleagues are treated worse and for many people the feel-good factor is absent.

All of these problems are interconnected. The weakness of our economy stems from the same sources as the divisions in our society.

- We have failed to cultivate the talents of our people. In a world where capital flows freely between countries, the living standards of ordinary people depend more than ever on the skills they have to offer. This should be obvious when three-quarters of our national income is earned by the skills of the workforce. Yet we have shamefully neglected the skills of half of our youngsters, and now we pay the penalty. Inequality has risen and this breeds crime.

- At the same time we have failed to keep our people in work. This partly reflects inadequate skills, but also our willingness to sweep unemployment under the carpet. We have encouraged dependency on benefits instead of helping everyone to be a functioning citizen.

- We have changed our tax and benefit rules so that the rich gain and the incomes of the poor fail to rise in line with incomes generally. Increasingly the poor are being marginalised. The whole public sector is subjected to ceaseless restructuring, and public sector professionals have become thoroughly demoralised – including major professions such as teachers, medics and civil servants. Contractual relationships are constantly introduced in place of relationships of trust.

- The same is true inside companies. Relationships

between colleagues have been soured by excessive restructuring and invidious pay formulae. We have encouraged a macho philosophy, in which downsizing has become a virility symbol. And many managers, over-concerned with deal-making or takeover threats, have become distracted from the task of developing their companies for the long term.

- The economy has been subjected to two of the five largest post-war recessions in the G7 countries. This has deeply undermined the confidence and security of our people. Many undertook large debts, believing in the Thatcher miracle, and now they are left with a sense of betrayal.

THE STAKEHOLDER PHILOSOPHY

What can we do to make things better, so that people feel they are getting what they should from life? The key is to take people seriously. Everyone should be able to make an effective contribution and get a fair share of what is produced. All should feel they are useful, that they are valued, that they have control over their lives. All should have a stake in society and in their work.

This is the vision of a stakeholder society – a society which aims at opportunity and fulfilment for all.[2] All the main proposals in this book are based on this idea.

- People need the skills to earn a decent living in an interesting job. The industries of the future will be increasingly knowledge-based. Without skills there is no hope for individuals, nor indeed is there any hope that Britain can exploit the new opportunities in the global market place. So we need a practical policy to ensure that every youngster gets a serious level of skill by the age of eighteen. And every adult needs a similar chance.

What Labour Can Do

- To be fulfilled, people need work. Unemployment causes pain which goes far beyond the simple loss of income. There are few pains worse than the pain of rejection. So we need to make it impossible for people to go on being rejected. There has to be a right to a job within a year of becoming unemployed (or sooner for the young). It can be done.

- We need a welfare state in which people have more control over their incomes – a more personalised pension and, for mothers, a better chance to earn a living rather than surviving on benefit. There are practical policies which can promote this.

- We need managers who will 'grow' their companies and develop the potential in their workers. The high-turnover society is not good for productivity or the nerves. A new framework for companies will help to promote stability and develop the potential of workers.

These are some of the key steps towards a stakeholder society, where all contribute and all receive a fair share. For too long it has been argued that greater inequality is an inevitable feature of a more successful society. In fact the evidence in Chapter 2 points in exactly the opposite direction. Successful societies are those in which everybody is able to make an effective contribution. Unequal societies fail to realise the potential of many of their citizens. Not surprisingly, stakeholder societies tend to have more rapid economic growth.

STABILITY AND EUROPE

Success also depends on good 'macroeconomic' management. If the economy lurches between boom and slump, that is bad for long-term growth and bad for the security of each one of us. In Britain macroeconomic management has been singularly inept for much of the last eighteen years.

- In this period, as stated, Britain has experienced two of the five deepest post-war recessions in any of the G7 industrial countries (see Table 1). This record of instability has hurt business investment and contributed to the sense of insecurity among workers.[3] Much of this unnecessary turbulence has come from excessive fluctuations in interest rates and in the value of the pound. In 1980, and again in 1990, the pound became excessively overvalued, making it impossible for many firms to compete in world markets – hence the recessions. The most natural way to avoid these shocks would be for us to join the single European currency in 1999. But this raises the whole question of Britain's role in the world.

- The Conservative government has been paralysed by its Euro-sceptic wing, so that Britain now has less and less influence in Europe. In the end we shall almost certainly join the single currency – but how much better to go in as a leader than to be dragged in screaming. Britain has a unique advantage in Europe through speaking the world language, and it is not too late for us to assume a leading role in Europe.

Table 1: The five biggest recessions since 1950 (G7 countries)

	Date	Percentage fall in GDP
Canada	1981–82	6.6
UK	**1979–81**	**6.0**
Italy	1974–75	5.5
USA	1974–75	4.0
UK	**1990–92**	**3.6**

CONCLUSION

These are the main economic issues for a Labour government. The aims are:

- prosperity through a high-skill, high-employment, dynamic economy

- fairness through a share for everyone

- security through a stable economy

A government cannot secure any of these things on its own. It can only provide the right framework and, where necessary, the money. But there are key levers. Labour should use them to:

- provide skills for everyone

- get people from welfare to work

- use public money to promote self-reliance

- get firms to go for long-term growth

- pursue responsible macroeconomic policies based on consensus

- join the European single currency

On all these issues the devil is in the detail. The policies will only work if the detail is convincing. If not, they are pious aspirations. So the main chapters in the book give detailed policies on each of these topics, backed up by evidence. If these policies are followed, they will go far to ensure that everybody has a stake in our society.

2

The Keys to Success

Nought's had, all's spent,
Where our desire is got without content.
                    Shakespeare

THE ONLY SOUND guide to economic policy is concrete evidence about what works well and what does not. So in this chapter we look first at how different countries with different policies have fared: how have they grown, and how widely have they spread the benefits of growth throughout the population?

Then we shall look more systematically at what causes economic growth. How do successful countries differ from the less successful? Is more inequality an inevitable by-product of faster growth? Was Mrs Thatcher right when she said at the Royal Geographical Society's 1991 presidential lecture, 'It's our job to glory in inequality'?

Finally, we shall look more deeply into human nature. Which features of the economy and society really affect people's happiness, and what does this tell us about the right priorities for a government wanting to improve people's lives?

BRITAIN

How is Britain doing? In the last eighteen years many things have improved. Most important, our managers have re-established their ability to run their firms. This may help to explain why, since 1979, our productivity has ceased to fall when compared to other European countries (see Figure 1). On the other hand, we have failed to make up any of the lost ground. As Figure 2 shows, our productivity growth since 1979 has been no better than that of our European competitors.[1] And, if anything, it has slowed down in the last eight years.

Many people are unaware of these facts, because the government usually focuses on manufacturing only – where our productivity growth since 1979 has indeed outshone the European average. But our employment in manufacturing has fallen so sharply that, despite productivity growth, our actual output in the sector has grown less than in most other countries.[2] And, in any case, manufacturing is a small part of the economy.

Our overall productivity record can only be described as disappointing. When one country has a lower income than another, that largely reflects obsolete technology and outdated practices, which can be put right by copying the richer countries. Thus, in general, poorer countries that follow good

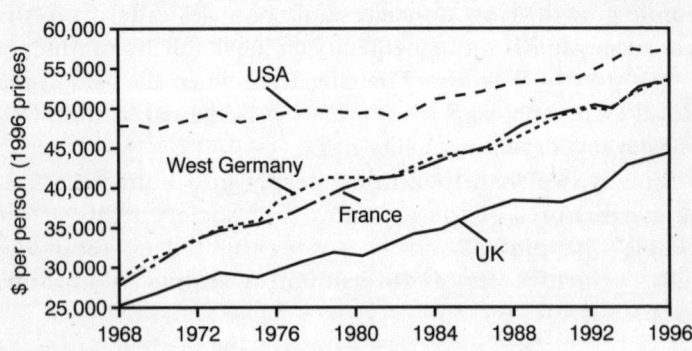

Figure 1: Production per person employed

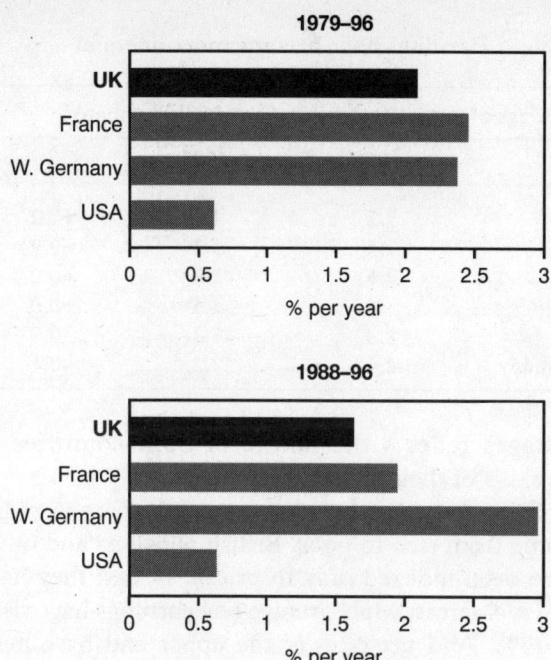

Figure 2: Productivity growth

policies catch up with richer countries – see for example the experience of Japan and South Korea. The fact that Britain is failing to catch up is a real disappointment, reflecting our lack of skills and the short-termist element in our management strategy.

At the same time Britain has become a deeply unequal society. Between 1979 and 1992, the living standards of the top 5% of Britons rose by 45% while those of the bottom 5% rose by under 15%.[3] We are now one of the most unequal countries in Europe.[4] The main reason for our increase in inequality is the increased disparity in wages. Britain and the United States are almost unique in the large increase they have had in wage inequality. This is shown for men in Table 2, and similar changes have happened for women. The increased

Table 2: Earnings have become more unequal

	Earnings of top 10% as ratio of bottom 10% (men)		
	1980	*1995*	*Change*
USA	3.2	4.3	+1.2
UK	2.4	3.3	+0.9
Japan	2.6	2.8	+0.2
France	3.4	3.4	+0.0
Sweden	1.2	1.2	0.0
West Germany	2.4	2.2	–0.1

spread of wages reflects the failure of both countries to develop the skills of their less able citizens.

On top of this there has been a weakened effort to redistribute income from rich to poor. British pensions and other benefits have been indexed only to prices, so that they have not grown in real terms, while average real earnings have risen by around 45%. And tax rates at the upper end have been slashed to a maximum rate of 40%.[5]

Another reason for increased inequality is the huge rise in unemployment (see Figure 3). Since the 1970s unemployment

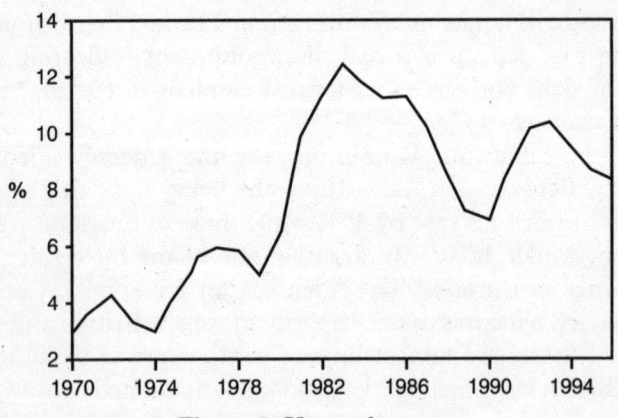

Figure 3: Unemployment

has risen in most European countries, though less in Germany than in many (see Figure 4). Twice in ten years unemployment in Britain has exceeded 10% of all workers. Since 1993 it has been falling: Britain had its recession earlier than the rest of Europe and is now having an earlier boom. But the unemployment problem has not gone away, and the feeling of insecurity continues.

Increased insecurity is also due to the new approach of British employers (see Figure 5). Increasingly they take people on for short-term contracts. Insecurity now affects white-collar as well as blue-collar workers – right up to the boardroom. Employers no longer scruple to sack workers,

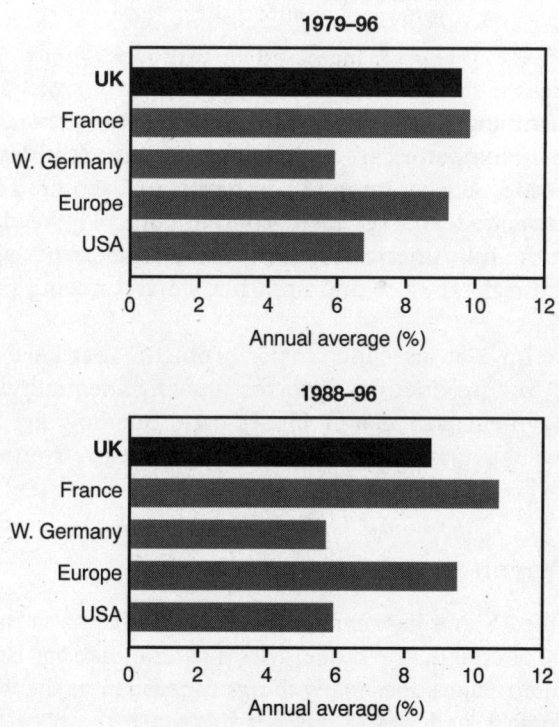

Figure 4: Unemployment

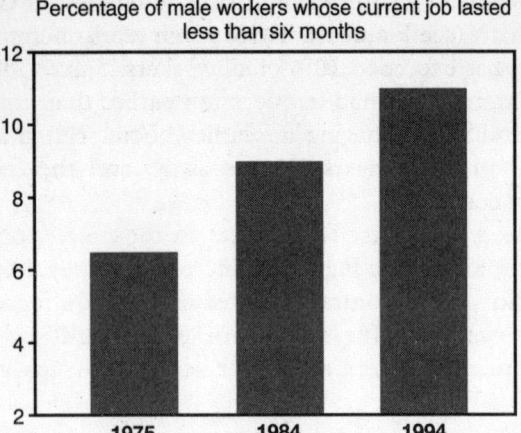

Figure 5: **Increased job turnover**

often justifying this by increased world competition, even when their companies are making good profits. Ruthless lay-offs are especially common in companies just acquired in the vastly expanded 'market for corporate control'. We do not yet have the full American system where the boss has almost unlimited right to 'hire and fire', but we are moving rapidly that way.

So we have at least four major problems that have to be tackled: low productivity growth; growing inequality; high unemployment and massive insecurity. But how are other countries like ours doing, and what can we learn from them?

THE UNITED STATES

The United States has many of the same problems as Britain, and was, of course, the model Mrs Thatcher had for Britain. The United States does many things superbly: it is the world's technological leader, and has been so since the turn of the century; its managers and professionals have a dynamism and professionalism which we should all copy; and their material standard of living is well above European levels. Women there have advanced further in the labour market than anywhere outside Scandinavia.

But the US is a low-growth country. Productivity is growing more slowly than in Europe, so that European living standards are steadily rising towards the US level.[6] At the same time US workers work very much longer hours than Europeans, and they generally have only two weeks' holiday a year. On the basis of output per hour worked, there is now no difference between the USA and the European core (France, West Germany, Benelux and Italy).[7]

What has gone wrong in America, and what should we learn from this? The answer is that America has failed to develop its less able workers. Even if we focus only on whites, the lowest-paid 10% of the American workforce now earn a real hourly wage 50% below that in western Germany and somewhat below that in Britain (see Figure 6). Not only are the poor worse off in America, but they are becoming poorer,

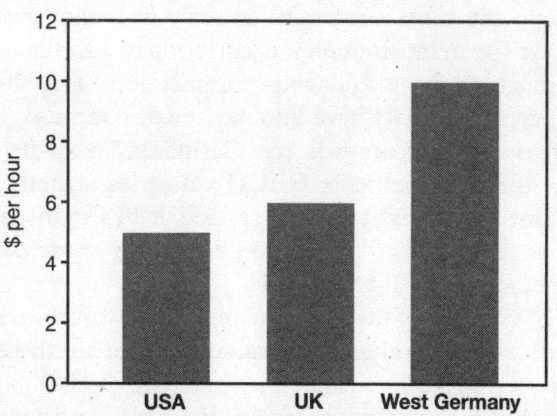

Figure 6: The lowest 10% of workers earn less in the USA than Europe

while in Europe their lot is improving.[8] These poor Americans are not the ones that most Britons meet. Their plight reflects partly a desperate educational failure in America, and partly the harshness of the American labour market and of American employers.

There is of course an up-side to this – unemployment in the US is comparatively low (see Figure 4).[9] Unemployment benefit there runs out after six months. After that you are on your own, with few government programmes to help. So, to live, you must work or engage in crime. Today 2% of American men are in jail – compared with 0.3% in Britain and even less in every other European country.[10] In the US another 5% are on parole or probation, and the numbers in jail have doubled in the last ten years.

So if we copied American labour market practice and American educational structures, we should end up with an underclass. If we want to avoid that, we have to find lessons to learn from elsewhere.[11] What of Europe and the Far East?

EUROPE

In Europe the most successful country in recent years has been West Germany, though it is currently in a difficult phase of the business cycle following reunification. The shock of that experience would have knocked most countries for six: reunification still costs western Germany 5% of its GDP, whereas the oil shock cost OECD countries a mere 2% of theirs. But Germany will recover, and it has many institutions that should be of interest to us – not for crude copying, but to get ideas about what works.

The basic ideas of the German approach, which are shared to a large extent in other European countries, are these:

- Equality is important for social cohesion, and requires a minimum standard of education and social provision for all. This implies substantial public expenditure.

- Workers should be treated by their employers as stakeholders and have well-defined employment rights.

- Managers should work for the long-term interests of their companies, and should aim at long-term relationships with their owners, financiers and suppliers. Hostile takeovers are virtually unknown.

- The social partners (employers, workers and government) should aim at a social consensus about social policy and pay.

How well is the model working? Germany has had good productivity growth compared with the US, and in the last eight years has averaged lower unemployment than the US. There are some clear elements of rigidity, which Germans recognise and which have been highlighted in the OECD Jobs Study (1994). So in some respects Germany will move its practices a little towards the British model. But this does not mean, as is often suggested, that we should not also move ourselves towards Germany – indeed, we have to do so. We have to learn from their framework of skills for all, from their long-term approach to business decisions, and from their consensus approach to pay.

THE FAR EAST

And what of the Far East – Japan, South Korea, Hong Kong, Singapore, Taiwan, Thailand and Malaysia? Most countries there have higher growth rates than either America or Europe. A part of this is simply the process of 'catching up'; poorer countries, if well governed, grow faster than rich ones. So Japan has already slowed down to the European level of productivity growth. But four other features stand out in these countries. First, they have a much higher level of education than other countries at the same income level, as the figures in

Table 3 illustrate.[12] That is one key to their rapid growth. A second feature is a high degree of self-discipline. Third, these countries have a rather equal distribution of income. All these features are highly relevant.

Table 3: Percentage of 13-year-olds able to multiply 9.2 times 2.5

Korea, Taiwan	70
France, Italy, Switzerland	55
England	13

In addition these countries have markedly lower tax rates than Europe or America. This is because social security is provided within the family. Income in old age comes from private savings (which are sometimes compulsory, as in Singapore). These savings in turn finance investment, which is also high because of high rates of return due to the possibilities of 'catch-up'.

There is no simple way in which we could follow the Far East model by drastically cutting back the state – cutting taxes in the hope that this would lead to a surge in investment and economic growth. We do not have the same family structure, nor the same possibilities for 'catch-up'. There are, however, lessons about the finance of pensions. But the main lessons from the Far East are the importance of education, self-discipline and social equality.

THE SOURCES OF ECONOMIC GROWTH

So there are lessons from everywhere – from the US about technological advance and progress for women, from Europe and the Far East about lifting the lives of all the people. But a *tour d'horizon* can only tell so much. We need more systematic knowledge about the causes of economic growth and dynamism, not from picking examples but from a systematic comparison including every country. This knowledge exists.[13]

Obviously there are many factors which contribute to growth. But what are the main ones? First, there is the point about catch-up: the richer the country already is, the harder it is to grow still richer, since there is less scope for copying the technology of others. Apart from this, countries grow faster in output per head

- the higher the skills of the workforce

- the more equal the levels of income

- the freer and more open their markets

- the more stable the economy

There is no clear evidence that the level of taxes affects the level of growth[14] – taxes can only be judged by the value of what they pay for.

These facts provide the basis for everything which follows in this book. Mrs Thatcher was wrong – inequality is *bad* for growth because it reflects underinvestment in skills and weakens the ability of the poor to improve themselves. This finding, which is based on many studies,[15] destroys the idea that inequality is the price of growth. Efficiency and equity are not (at the most general level) contradictory goals. In some contexts they are,[16] but, at the strategic level, when a society is setting its institutions, we can and should aim at both growth and equity.

This is a very important finding. For when we think about the good society, we worry not only about how much people have on average, but about how it is distributed. We know that an extra pound means more to a poor person than to a rich one[17] – so we would always prefer a more equal society unless greater equality was bound to reduce the average income available. It is therefore a relief to find that there *are* policies which are both good for growth and good for equality.

HUMAN NATURE AND THE GOOD SOCIETY

However, when we think about the good society, we know that it requires a lot more than high (and equal) incomes. Britain has become very much richer in the last twenty years, yet surveys show that people are no more satisfied with their lives (see Figure 7). And in this respect Britain and the US have been doing worse than most European countries (see Table 4).

So what do we know about which aspects of society make people feel satisfied with life? Obviously income matters, otherwise why do people play the Lottery?[18] But you want a lot else – above all to feel that you belong, that you are needed, and that you can control your life.

At work you want harmonious relations with your colleagues. If others get incomes which you consider unfair, this reduces your own satisfaction. That is why some forms of performance-related pay create such bad feeling.[19] Even if they enhance productivity a bit, they may not be worth it in terms of the total welfare of employees and owners. People

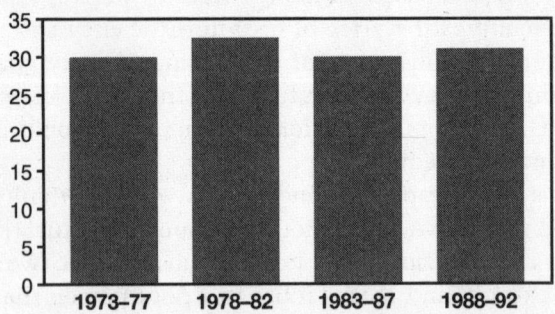

Figure 7: Percentage reporting themselves as 'very satisfied' with their lives

Table 4: Percentage reporting themselves as 'very satisfied' with their lives

Increased since 1970s	*Decreased since 1970s*
France	UK
Germany	Ireland
Italy	Belgium
Netherlands	USA
Denmark	
Luxembourg	

prefer relationships of co-operation and trust to purely contractual relationships – which often highlight the conflicts of interest between people and groups. Within working organisations we need to restore the sense of fraternity, and stop the constant encroachment of market-based relationships. Between one firm and another the market can work wonders. But the encroachment of the market into every cranny will ultimately undo the glue which holds society together and gives pleasure to life.

Happiness also depends on having work, if that is what you want.[20] Unemployment is one of the greatest sources of misery. According to one study, people are more unhappy (other things being equal) if they are unemployed than if they are 'separated, divorced or widowed'. Figure 8 compares the average levels of distress for people who are unemployed with people who are in work. Similar differences in distress are found when the same person moves between work and unemployment.[21]

Becoming unemployed reduces a person's happiness more than a major loss of income. So the good society must do more than maximising the total national income. It should be ready, if necessary, to sacrifice some income in order to reduce unemployment. However, this should *not* be necessary, since most sensible policies to reduce unemployment will also increase total income. But this argument reinforces the view that cutting unemployment must be a top priority.

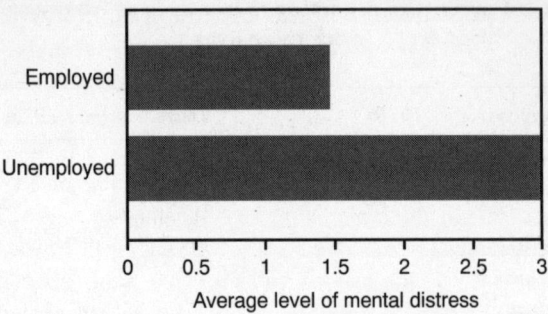

Figure 8: Unemployment and mental distress

Then there is the need for security. Even for the employed, security is a major priority. People's confidence has been severely dented by the recessions of the last twenty years, and by the generally increased insecurity of employment.

Crime flourishes when unemployment is high and when incomes are unequal – the evidence here is clear.[22] So if we reduce unemployment and inequality we should also reduce crime.

But there is more to crime than that. We have become a less disciplined society; suiting yourself has become increasingly acceptable. We have been infiltrated by the American idea that we must 'have it all'. It is not surprising that school discipline has steadily deteriorated, to the point where British children visiting French schools are shocked by the atmosphere of order and hard work which prevails. The worst-behaved schools in the world are now in Britain and the USA, and the social prestige of teachers is lower in those countries than elsewhere.

We need to rebuild a society based on mutual obligations, where people acknowledge responsibilities for others as well as themselves. This needs to influence all aspects of life – in work, school and family as well as government. Through the government, society has to accept responsibility for those who cannot help themselves, while at the same time those who *can* help themselves do so without expecting handouts from the rest of us.

CONCLUSION

We need a society that is both dynamic and decent – and such a society *is* possible. The key features of a good society are: prosperity, fairness and comradeship, full employment, and security. To achieve these objectives, the government's main levers are: the provision of skills, the treatment of unemployment, welfare reform, the business framework, and macroeconomic policy.

We turn now to each of these policy areas individually. We treat them in some detail, to see what would actually work and what would not.

Summary

- *Since 1979 productivity in Britain has grown no faster than in the richer countries of Northern Europe. This is disappointing because a country with lower productivity should grow faster than those which are nearer the technological frontier.*

- *Britain and the US have also experienced a huge increase in inequality. In the US the poorer workers have experienced steady falls in real income, and the bottom tenth of US whites now earn 50% less than the bottom tenth in Germany.*

- *The US has avoided high unemployment through the harshness of its welfare system, but its educational failures have produced an underclass – with 7% of US men in jail or on parole or probation.*

- *By giving skills to (nearly) all, western Germany has achieved over the last eight years both lower unemployment and more equality than the USA. Other significant features of the German model are a longer-term approach in business, and a more consensual approach to wages.*

- *The experience of the Far East confirms the importance of education in economic growth. These countries have high rates of saving, partly because of good investment opportunities (due to catch-up) and partly because much social security is provided by the family rather than the state. These countries are much more equal than the US.*

- *There is thus clear evidence that inequality is not a necessary condition for growth. In fact growth is fostered by a high general educational level for all. Thus it is clearly feasible to seek more growth* and *greater equality.*

- *Over the last twenty years people in Britain and the US have not become more satisfied with their lives, unlike people in most European countries. This may be due to the growth of inequality, insecurity and divisive forms of performance-related pay.*

- *Unemployment is a major source of misery which goes far beyond the pain of income loss. Cutting unemployment is therefore a major instrument for raising welfare.*

- *A good society provides prosperity, fairness, full employment and security. The instruments to achieve these objectives are: the provision of skills, better approaches to unemployment, welfare reform, better incentives for long-term growth in business, and a stable economy. These are the topics we address in the rest of the book.*

3

A Skills Revolution

Knowledge itself is power.
Francis Bacon

THREE QUARTERS OF the nation's income is earned by labour, and the main factor which determines those earnings is skill. Countries which have higher levels of skill grow faster than other countries at the same level of income.[1]

Britain's policy on skills cannot be passive: to simply wait until manifest shortages appear. It must be active: to improve skill levels and thus produce in advance a more flexible workforce, better equipped to respond to and initiate change. The stark reality is that the demand for low-skilled labour is falling rapidly. Muscle-power has become largely useless; it is brain-power which is needed. This is perhaps the greatest problem facing industrial societies. The future of millions will depend on whether we can reduce the supply of unskilled people faster than the demand collapses. If we fail to do so, we shall face mass unemployment.

But how fast an upgrading is needed? This must depend critically on how well we are already doing. In higher education Britain is doing pretty well – we have a system to rival any in the world. But in schools and in vocational training we are doing less well. If you are bright, you generally get a good education, but if you are below average you get a much worse deal than in other European countries or in the Far East. In fact the way in which we treat the weaker third of our youngsters is a national scandal, made more dangerous by the relentless fall in the demand for low-skilled labour.

So the top priority for educational policy is to raise the minimum standards for all young people. We need policies, described below, which will ensure that all youngsters achieve proper literacy and numeracy before they leave primary school *and* a basic level of professional skill before they reach adulthood. Educational reform should be focused around the achievement of these two key objectives.

THE RECORD

To see the scale of the problem, we have only to compare the qualifications which our youngsters achieve with those of youngsters on the Continent or the Far East. To have any reasonable skill, a young person must have either five GCSEs at Grade C or above, or an 'equivalent' professional qualification, for example a City and Guilds Part 2 in bricklaying. Generically, this whole level is called Level 2 – meaning that it is equivalent to NVQ2 (National Vocational Qualification 2). In Britain nearly 40% of our youngsters never reach this minimal level.[2]

The government recently published an analysis of how this compared with the performance of youngsters in five of our competitor countries. The result is shown in Figure 9. Only in the USA is the situation remotely similar to ours. We have twice as many unqualified people as Germany and France.

If instead we look at the upper end of the spectrum, Britain is doing fine. As Figure 9 shows, we have almost as many people getting degrees as anywhere else. But the lower we come down, the worse our performance. If we take the next

A Skills Revolution

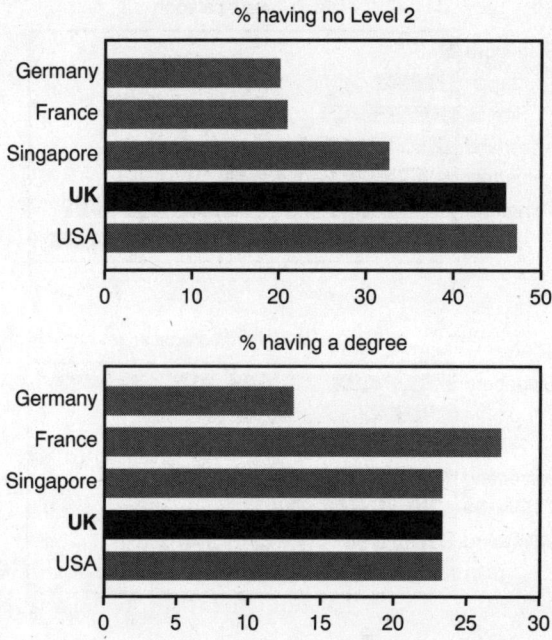

Figure 9: Too many people without a skill

level down (Level 3), which means GCE A-level or equivalent, Germany has almost 75% of young adults who have reached that level, while Britain has only 36%. But France, Singapore and the USA are in a similar situation to Britain. It is when we reach the lowest level that Britain and the USA do so much worse than the others. We are really failing the bottom 40% of our population.

The failure to equip our young people with vocational skills reflects in part the failure of our schools to prepare them earlier on. This is especially true in mathematics. Figure 10 shows the results of the latest standard international comparison of maths achievement at the age of fourteen. The results

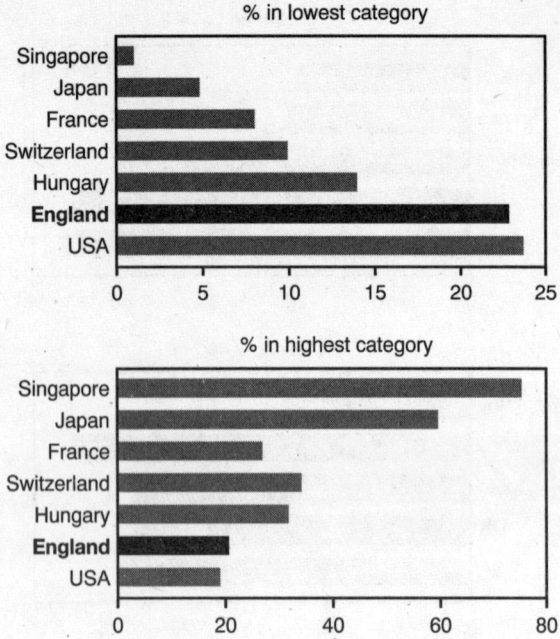

Figure 10: Too many with poor maths

are devastating. England and the USA have *twice* as many people in the bottom category of achievement as the other countries, and even at the top end we are not very strong.

These objective tests are reflected in the perceptions of international businessmen. One survey asked multinational companies what they thought about the basic skills of youngsters entering employment (see Figure 11). On both literacy and numeracy, but especially numeracy, Britain ranked low. Broadly speaking, the reading standards of British teenagers have improved little since 1945.[3]

The research of Sigmund Prais and others has shown why other countries are so much more successful than we are with

A Skills Revolution

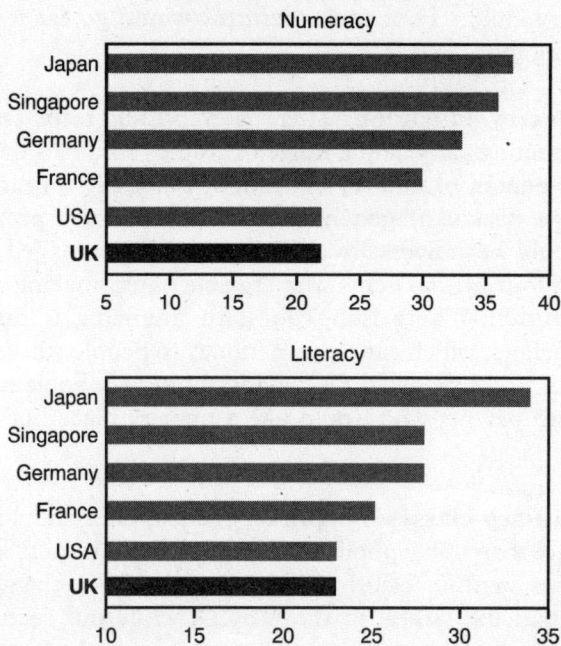

Figure 11: Multinational companies' rating of basic skills

lower-ability children.[4] They have much clearer objectives for the achievements of children at each age, and they expect all children to meet them. They teach the whole class as a single group for more of the time, rather than letting each child proceed at their own pace. They do not accept a long tail of low achievement as a fact of nature, and they are less inclined to glory in 'diversity' than has become fashionable in Britain.

LITERACY AND NUMERACY

Our first objective must be to make sure that every child leaves primary school with functional literacy and numeracy (unless they have severe learning difficulties). What the average child can now do at eleven should become the minimum for every child.[5] Four major reforms would go far towards achieving this.

- **Nursery education**. There is everything to be said for beginning early, and a range of studies confirms the lasting benefit of nursery education, especially for children from disadvantaged homes.[6] Thus nursery provision should be universally available for children aged three and four, with parents who are able to pay making a contribution. There is no point in financing it through vouchers, which simply give money to people whose children are already in fee-paying nursery schools and to other parents who would like a nursery place but could pay.

- **Primary classes**. No primary school class should have more than thirty pupils. At present Britain is quite anomalous in this regard. Our primary school classes are among the largest in the OECD, while our secondary school classes are around the average.[7] If we look at pupils per teacher, we have ratios of 22:1 in primary schools and 16:1 in secondary schools (similar to the position in further and higher education).[8] One might have thought that the older the person, the more they could study on their own. Clearly the priority for extra teachers is in primary schools – especially for younger children as they take their first key steps. Eliminating classes of over thirty for five- to seven-year-olds would cost £70 million – an essential first move.[9] We should also encourage a wider use of experienced 'helpers' to work under teachers' supervision in infant schools.

- **The teaching profession**. Perhaps the most important reform of all is to raise the standards and standing of the teaching profession. These two aspects go hand in hand. Everyone acknowledges that there are some teachers who ought not to be teaching. This spells disaster for some children and brings disrepute on schools and the profession in general. The profession needs, like other professions, to have control over its own membership through a General Teaching Council, analogous to the General Medical Council for doctors. This would certify people as fit to teach, and strike them off if they are not. There should be separate certification for primary and secondary schools, and separate certificates to teach mathematics. A date should be fixed after which (as on the Continent) you could not teach mathematics without a certificate of competence, and you would need a different certificate for teaching it at primary and secondary levels. If this were done, there would have to be a massive programme of re-training and of training new recruits. A similar procedure is needed for people considered fit to be head teachers.

Teacher training also needs to be reformed. Too many teachers get their first experience of teaching in bad schools. They never really learn to cope and their sights become permanently lowered. It is like trying to climb Everest before you have climbed Snowdon. Instead we need some highly professional schools, rather like the 'teaching hospitals' in the medical profession, where trainee teachers can learn best practice in a controlled environment. These schools would be linked to universities. Teaching in such 'teaching schools' should be an integral part of teacher training, and only those who can perform properly there on a continuous basis should be admitted to the profession. There have already been some experiments along these lines, but they need generalising. Such 'teaching schools' would become seed-beds for educational improvement, and remedy the present situation where most educational change is imposed on schools from outside rather than being developed within the teaching profession itself.

- **School organisation**. Whatever happens, unless schools have the right internal organisation, some pupils will slip through the net and the 'first objective' will not be achieved. There must be a mechanism which makes everyone, teacher and pupil, realise that they have got to achieve the basic standard by the age of eleven.

  Until the Second World War, the mechanism was the need to 'pass out' from each grade before you could go into the grade above it. This remains the practice on much of the Continent. Those few who do not, say one in thirty, repeat the year. In this way all the children in a class work to master the same material – though many will go beyond it. There is much to be said for an arrangement along these lines.

A SKILL FOR EVERY YOUNGSTER[10]

The ultimate goal is that every young person should acquire a basic professional skill before they lose touch with the educational system. It is no good leaving this to employers. The evidence is clear: employers only provide training to those who already have a basic level of skill. For example, in spring 1994 the proportion of employees who got some training in the month before they were surveyed was around 25% for university graduates, but under 5% for people with no qualification.[11]

It is no good simply blaming employers for this state of affairs, as many people do, since if an employer gives someone a basic training, there is no way to stop the trained person leaving and working for another employer who needs the same skill. This freedom to move is an inescapable part of a free society. But it has a clear implication. Where skills are 'general', that is, of value to many employers, they have to be financed collectively. It is only where the skills are 'company-specific' that employers can be sure of trapping the return to their investment in skills, and it is only then that we can and should rely on employers to provide the skills.

British employers have become better and better at providing this 'company-specific' training – the proportion of workers who 'got some training in the month before the survey' nearly doubled between 1984 and 1994. But general skills are a quite different issue. Here is a case where the free market does not deliver. Individual employers have no incentive to invest. And although the individual student does have some incentive, it is inadequate.

The reasons are obvious. An individual student is enormously uncertain about what the return to his investment will be, even though to society as a whole the average return on education is relatively certain. Moreover, when education raises a person's income, the government takes away a part of the return in higher taxes. From the point of view of companies as a whole, there are benefits from a large pool of educated workers, but no individual will take this into account when he decides whether to get educated. And finally, the whole of society will suffer if we have a large pool of uneducated workers – through higher unemployment benefits, for example. This matters to society, but a young person or a company cannot be expected to take it into account. These are powerful reasons why the state should pay to get all its youngsters up to a basic level of skill – and, if possible, even further.

The basic minimum for all should be set at Level 2, and should include the key skills of numeracy, literacy and information technology. (The current government target of 75% of youngsters achieving this target by the year 2000 is quite inadequate.[12]) Every young person should regard this level as a minimum condition for proper citizenship. To get everyone up to this standard, five main changes are needed:

- Everyone under eighteen who has not reached this

standard should be working for it – on a part-time or full-time basis. This will involve at least a day a week of off-the-job vocational education in, for example, a college of further education. As now, this would be paid for by the state.

- Anyone employing someone under eighteen should make sure they get this education for at least a day a week, unless they have reached Level 2. This will of course be a real constraint on employers who currently employ young people in dead-end jobs. Indeed some employers will stop employing youngsters if they have to be released for a day a week. If so, however, that is better in the long-run than having those young people entering adult life with no skill. A person's whole approach to life is influenced by whether they have a clear idea of what it is to be a professional person, and to take pride in their expertise. We can only instil this idea if all young people, be they in factories, building sites, shops or hotels, are given an idea of what it is to achieve a serious level of skill in a particular area.

- Where young people cannot find employers willing to hire them, they will have to get their Level 2 qualification full-time – so that they can then get a serious job. This would normally take 6–12 months, except for youngsters whose school performance has been so bad that they first need a remedial course in further education before tackling Level 2.

- One way to deal with the school problem is to let young people start on their vocational education at the age of fourteen, while still in school. For many of them this would provide better motivation than hanging around doing little until they can leave school. If young people realise that 'you have got to get your Level 2' before you can stop studying, many of them would opt to start on a vocational qualification at age fourteen. It should be a free choice – no one should be forced to do it, nor get streamed into it. While at school, these young people would be studying for a Level 2 professional qualification, which would take half a day a week (or sometimes a whole day).[13] It should be made possible for them to spend this time in a college if they want to do a subject which cannot be taught in school – like building, for example. This proposal, already advocated by the present government, would not shunt people into a dead-end vocational track. From Level 2 there is a route up through Level 3 to university, if people want it and have the aptitude.

- To bring all this about, young people will need guidance and monitoring. They will need to see a careers adviser every year between the ages of fourteen and eighteen, who will make sure that they are not slipping through the net. This will require a new, more tightly focused Careers Service, more visible and brought back more firmly under public control. It will be the pivotal instrument for making the skills revolution happen.

These changes have been proposed by the Labour Party under the title Target 2000, meaning that by the year 2000 every youngster under eighteen who does not have Level 2 must be studying for it either full- or part-time. If it happens, this will be a huge change. Something like 350,000 extra young people will be studying for Level 2 (perhaps half full-time and half part-time). At the same time the existing programme called Youth Training will be abolished: only half of trainees obtain any qualification and very few get to Level 2. Youth Training has been of variable quality, and trainees have often failed to receive the help and supervision they needed.

Some people question whether there should be any new initiative at the 16–18 stage until the schools have been put right. One should reject that line of thought. We cannot abandon the current teenagers. And, even in the future, 16–18 will be a key stage where people are making the transition from school to work. It is crucial that they get an understanding then of what a skill is, and of its importance in the workplace – as well as a last chance to get basic skills when they can see how important these are in the work environment.

One further point. At present you can get an NVQ2 simply by being able to perform a set of tasks without any real understanding of why one procedure is better than another. The approach is solely competence-based (knowing how), with very little cognitive element (knowing why). This needs reforming. As I have said, all young people should be able to demonstrate that they have key skills in literacy, numeracy and information technology. But they also need some extra knowledge about their own profession. Both these features can be provided within the framework of the so-called General NVQ2 – or GNVQ2. This qualification provides key skills as well as knowledge relevant to work in a particular sector. It also includes a range of options which should be extended to include the very specific practical skills now provided by the NVQ2.[14] Reformed in this way, GNVQ2 would be the basic Level 2 qualification achieved by all those who do not do well in GCSE. To be fully credible, the GNVQ (and NVQ) systems need a bigger element of external examination than they have at present. Ultimately only youngsters with at least GNVQ2 or good GCSEs should be considered to have reached Level 2.

APPRENTICESHIPS

We have focused so far on the most important objective: to get every child literate and numerate by the age of eleven, and up to a reasonable skill level by eighteen. But Level 2 is a very basic level of skill. Most people should go well beyond this. At present most education beyond this level is what is sometimes called 'academic'. This is a misnomer, for it includes a huge element of vocational education – in law, medicine, accountancy, business studies, teaching, nursing studies and the like. It is better described as 'academically-oriented', and is generally full-time. This whole sector is very well developed in Britain.

What is dreadfully lacking is experience-based part-time education above Level 2. The government, having allowed the apprenticeship system to die of neglect in the 1980s, is now trying hard to resurrect it. But so far Modern Apprenticeships only cover some 60,000 youngsters. One reason for this is that there are not enough potential recruits of interest to employers. Most employers want a Level 2 qualification, and at present most of those who get Level 2 get good GCSEs and continue in full-time education. Once we have overcome the Level 2 bottleneck, we need to see a major expansion of Level 3 apprenticeships – to produce the trained technicians, supervisors and office staff for the new information age.[15]

Much of the development will occur spontaneously if Modern Apprenticeships are allowed to expand with adequate financial support. The most important area to develop is the commercial apprenticeship. In Germany most businessmen have done such an apprenticeship. Some do it after getting their 'A-levels', spending two years as, say, a Deutsche Bank trainee; and then, with relevant experience under their belt, they go on to a degree in business. Others start their apprenticeships when they are younger, and generally do not go on to university. The results of this system are evident in the success of German business, and Britain needs a major development in this kind of business training.

Raising the skill level of the workforce is an integral part of raising the performance of our economy. If we demand higher standards of companies, they will have to demand higher standards of their workers. Industry associations have an important role to play here. For example, the electrical contracting industry and the travel agent industry insist that their members employ workers who satisfy certain skill requirements. The rest of the economy would benefit greatly if other industry associations did the same.

This whole process means that we will have to use the part-time route as a major method of improving the skills of our workforce. We need a big expansion of part-time education at Level 3.

But who will pay for it? At present there is a huge anomaly in our system of educational finance. Up to the age of nineteen, education is, in principle, paid for by the state.[16] But after that there are fees, unless you are clever enough to get on to a degree-level course. If you do this full-time, you pay no fees and generally get some maintenance, but if you do a sub-degree course, you pay the fee.

This is outrageously unfair. University students have already had free full-time education for their A-levels, while those who left school early and now want to study for the same level of education have to pay, even if they are only studying part-time.

No wonder that sub-degree vocational education has withered on the vine. Successive governments (especially since 1979) have looked after the middle-class interest by shelling out billions on full-time academically-oriented education, while constantly pushing vocational education to pay for itself. This is both unfair and economically inefficient. It will have to be changed.

All education for nationally recognised qualifications at sub-degree level should be free, just as A-levels in sixth forms are free. A natural approach would be to continue charging fees, but for the state to pay the fee through Labour's proposed Individual Learning Accounts.

At present further education colleges collect about £300 million in fees (about half from firms and half from individuals).[17] This money would now have to be found from public funds, plus the cost of the educational expansion triggered off by the no-fee regime: perhaps a total cost of £750 million. How can this money be found, together with the costs of the other improvements I have been discussing?

UNIVERSITY FINANCE

A lot of it will have to come from the most privileged sector, the universities. University graduates get paid much more on average than other members of the community (see Table 5), and current research confirms that most of the difference is in fact a result of the education they received.[18] The education is an investment, and it yields a return. The rest of society gets a good part of the return in higher taxes and other social advantages, and therefore should be willing to provide a subsidy of the same size as these 'external' benefits. But when the cost exceeds the benefits to the rest of society the students should pay, with the help of a proper student-friendly loan scheme.

So what is the appropriate subsidy? This question is being investigated by the high-powered Dearing Committee set up by agreement between the government and the Labour Party to look into the whole future of higher education. I will only suggest some broad ideas. The appropriate subsidy would cover most (but perhaps not all) of the tuition cost, that is, the

Table 5: Educated people earn more

(Average annual earnings of full-time employees aged over 21, 1995, £)

Graduates	23,400
A-level	18,300
Other Level 3 qualifications	17,900
Level 2 qualifications	15,600
No Level 2 qualification	13,200
All	16,900

cost of providing the teaching. It would not cover the student's cost of living, so university students would have to look after their own living expenses, plus, perhaps, in due course a smallish fee.

If students have to pay more than they do now, they will have to borrow to pay for it. We therefore need a new form of student loan scheme – call it a Learning Bank – that will provide loans in the way least likely to discourage students. This means two things: repayment must be linked to subsequent income and it must be collected in the most painless way.[19]

If a person is on a low income they should automatically repay over a longer period. How long? Suppose for example that a student has borrowed £16,000 by the end of his course, and that the scheme says you have to repay 1% of your annual income for each £4,000 borrowed, until you have repaid the loan. The rate of interest is 1% above base rate. Then, if the student subsequently earns an average graduate salary, he will repay in twenty-four years. If he earns 25% above the average, he will repay in nineteen years and if he earns 25% below the average he will repay in thirty-two years.[20] It is also essential that the repayment be as automatic as possible. It should therefore be collected by direct withholding at source – together with the National Insurance contribution.

But, one might ask, how does this help with the government's immediate financing problem, since the repayments come in much later than the original borrowing? The answer is that the money for the loan has to come from the private sector. This can be arranged quite simply. The Learning Bank would be an independent body offering loans under government regulations. Students would take on repayment obligations and the Learning Bank would auction these obligations to the private sector on the financial markets. Owing to the risk of default, the financial markets might not be willing to pay exactly the face value of the loan, and the state would meet the difference.[21] But this would be small.

This new approach to university funding will release a lot

of public money which can be used to finance education and training at lower levels. At present, student maintenance costs the Exchequer some £2 billion a year.[22] The cost of teaching in universities is £5 billion,[23] so if 20% was taken in fees that would release another £1 billion. Obviously all of this withdrawal of money will have to be phased in carefully, and within the next five years it is difficult to see more than the elimination of student maintenance grants.

This leaves one major issue. Not all universities are the same, but (except for Oxford and Cambridge)[24] they all get their public money per student according to the same formula. The formula allows more for universities with strong lines of research, but even so it is becoming increasingly difficult for the more research-based universities to maintain their standards. The overall state funding for universities is being cut, and by 1998 funding per student will have fallen by nearly 40% over a ten-year period.[25]

For too long there have been no universities in Britain which can compete with the top universities in the US, like Harvard, MIT, Chicago, Stanford and Princeton. And we now win fewer and fewer Nobel prizes in this country. To be fair, this is a European rather than exclusively British problem. Intellectual leadership has largely passed to the US, and this is seriously damaging to the economies of Europe.

Britain here has a unique opportunity, with our tradition of high-quality higher education and, above all, our language – which is already the world language of information technology and rapidly becoming the world language in general. (Ninety per cent of youngsters in Europe now learn it as their first foreign language.) This gives us an enormous advantage. If the US, with a population of around 250 million, can produce a dozen great universities, Europe with around 700 million people can do the same, and many of them can be in Britain.

Higher education is already one of Britain's great export industries, earning over £1 billion in foreign exchange, and it has the potential for rapid growth. The potential demand from both Europe and Asia is vast, and it exists at all points on the quality spectrum. Foreigners are willing to pay.

But what about the British government's contribution? This is not at present enough to support any leading world universities in Britain, and it is currently programmed to fall. If we want to have any world-class universities the government will have to provide more support, or these universities will have to charge extra 'top-up' fees.

Closely related is the issue of research funding. Research is vital for the dynamism of an economy and a society. But we spend less on research in higher education (relative to our working population) than any other major country except Japan – about one third less than the average for Germany, Italy, Holland and the USA.

Thus we need a judicious increase in funding for both pure and applied research. The government is right to insist that much research should be clearly relevant to wealth-creation. But the biggest changes in human wealth were produced by the pure logic of scientific discovery; it is this which uncovered the properties of electricity, materials and the workings of the human body.

LIFELONG LEARNING

So far we have focused on education for young people. But education should be a lifelong process, with people updating their skills as they move into new work, or as human knowledge expands. Moreover there are many people who missed out on their education when they were young; for them lifelong learning includes a process of catching up.

These thoughts are commonplace, but very little is done to implement them. The main reason is finance. Very little has been done to help people with the costs of studying later in life. Three steps are essential.

- All sub-degree courses leading to recognised national

qualifications should be free, regardless of age. This simple change would open a window of opportunity to all adults. The rationale for it is quite simple. We have public finance for education because of the benefits which the rest of society gains when a person gets educated. These benefits do not depend on whether the person who studied was an adult or a youngster, nor whether they studied part-time or full-time. The first step to providing wider educational entitlements is simply to make education for sub-degree qualifications free.[26]

- But many adults also have difficulty financing their living costs when studying. The Learning Bank should therefore be able to make loans to students of any age over eighteen doing courses leading to recognised qualifications.

- Some adults would also like to save up in advance for a course, especially if their employers would contribute in a reciprocal way. This is certainly desirable, and such contributions should be tax-exempt at the time when the saving is made. For simplicity all such saving should go into an Individual Learning Account at the Learning Bank. These accounts could also be the channel for paying the state's contribution to tuition costs.[27]

At every level of education the basic principle should be that laid down by the Robbins Committee: education should be available for all who want it and are qualified to benefit from that level of education. The only rider is that they make the necessary financial contribution. But there should be no rationing of places.

Educational technology

A skills revolution can only happen through a massive increase in enrolments in sub-degree level courses. This will be enormously expensive, unless we can find more efficient ways of educating people. The technology of education has barely changed since the century after Caxton established the first printing press in England. Basically we depend on the live teacher and the printed word for our knowledge about standard course material. That is not how we get our knowledge about current affairs, business or the performing arts; this mainly comes through TV, radio, tapes, films, videos, CD-ROMS and now the Internet. In fact the Army and business have for a long time used films, videos and now computer programs as routine methods of instruction. Only the educational system will not budge.

In the 1960s Britain established the Open University, which has been by far the most successful distance-learning institution in the world. Its teaching deploys TV, radio, correspondence, and high-quality programmed texts. But the rest of the universities have changed their methods very little. As cost pressures develop, they will have to. It is absurdly costly to have a hundred lecturers in different universities preparing and delivering their own courses in introductory economics, and cost pressures will open the way for greater use of high-quality materials bought in from outside.

But the most obvious place for high-quality package courses is at sub-degree level. The market is even larger, making for greater economies of scale, and the materials are more suited to standard presentation. It is critically urgent to develop good high-quality packages for the new courses at Levels 2 and 3, and to find ways of delivering them to the whole range of potential students.

This should be the prime objective for the University for Industry which Labour is proposing. This new organisation should have two main responsibilities:

- It should stimulate through small amounts of 'seedcorn' finance the production of high-quality sub-degree level teaching packages – on CD-ROM, video, paper and the like. These should be available to regular providers in colleges and elsewhere, as well as through distance learning.

- The University of Industry should develop its own framework for delivering these packages directly to homes and workplaces, drawing heavily on the experience of the Open University, but using the new forms of cable and satellite transmission now available. Every workplace with over fifty workers should have a learning centre linked to the Internet. However, it would be a mistake for the University for Industry to award its own qualifications. We have enough qualifications as it is: what we need is more students to get them.

BROADER A-LEVELS

There is one further point that affects the whole of our education system: the fact that our educated classes in Britain are highly segmented.

- The worst feature is that so many of them are virtually innumerate. This is true from primary school teachers to journalists to cabinet ministers. They have no sense of orders of magnitude nor the command of basic ideas like correlation.

- On the other side there are people with a science or engineering training who are quite unable to write a clear report in English.

- Third, an amazing number of people have no idea about commerce or how the business system works. This contributes to the continuing anti-commercial bias in our culture. British businessmen, other than bankers, tend to be less analytical than in other countries, and fewer of them are as artistically cultivated as in Europe.

Many of these problems stem from our highly specialised educational system. Nowhere else in the world can you give up maths at sixteen and then go on to university. Believe it or not, only 5–6% of our young people now study serious mathematics beyond the age of sixteen. Nor is there any other country where someone doing science at university could have studied no non-science subject since sixteen.

Ever since the 1950s there have been campaigns for broader A-levels. In 1988 the Higginson Report recommended a fundamental reform involving much more breadth.[28] Though broadly supported by the universities, it was rejected by the government. More recently, the Dearing Report (1996) recommended that a broad set of A-levels should be given a special title – but it is unlikely that universities will encourage many people to go for this. One major problem is that university science departments insist that they cannot teach to degree standard unless people come to university with three science A-levels. If not, they say, they will have to lengthen the university course to four years.

The best approach is gradual reform. I would suggest the following as a first step: universities should insist that A-level students have at least an A/S level in maths *and* at least one A/S level in an arts or social science. This would be a major step forward, and a practical one.

CONCLUSION

Millions of people in Britain today are not making the most of their abilities. By the time they are fully adult, they realise it; when they are young, they ignore the risks. The state has a duty to young people to help them make the most of their potential.

Our obligation is especially to those whose potential is

A Skills Revolution

limited. We must ensure that everyone without severe learning difficulties reaches at least a basic skill before they are launched into adult life. That means starting early. But it also means keeping opportunities open into adult life. It is truly scandalous that an able youngster can get five years of free full-time tuition after the age of sixteen, while a less able one gets (if lucky) a few years' part-time education up to nineteen before his education becomes fee-paying. Both fairness and efficiency demand that we shift some of the public help away from the most privileged and towards the larger part of our people, whose talents are now so undeveloped. This does not require a complicated system of educational entitlements, with vouchers or the like. It just needs easy access.

Summary

- *By the age of eleven every child should be literate and numerate, and by eighteen every youngster should have a Level 2 skill.*

- *Nursery education should be available for every child aged three and four; where they can, parents could contribute towards the cost.*

- *Primary school classes of over thirty should be eliminated, beginning with children aged five to seven.*

- *Teaching should become a fully self-regulating profession with a General Teaching Council which controls who can teach, including specific qualifications required to teach mathematics at primary and secondary level.*

- *Any youngster who has not achieved a Level 2 skill should have to study for it either full- or part-time up to at least eighteen. Anyone employing youngsters under eighteen would have to release them for a day-a-week off-the-job vocational education (where the cost was paid by the state). This so-called Target 2000 should be in operation by the year 2000.*

- *Youngsters in school could start work for a professional Level 2 qualification from fourteen onwards, alongside their GCSE.*

- *The Careers Service should take on a new responsibility of interviewing every youngster once a year between the ages of fourteen and eighteen, to ensure that they were on course for Level 2.*

- *All sub-degree education leading to recognised national qualifications should be paid for by the state – for youngsters and adults alike.*

A Skills Revolution

- *Degree students should pay their own living costs, like most other students, and in due course perhaps a small standard tuition fee.*

- *To make all this possible, there would be a massive programme of student loans through the Learning Bank. Repayment would be related to eventual income, and collected automatically together with National Insurance.*

- *Lifelong learning among adults will be encouraged by free education for sub-degree level qualifications and by the provision of loans from the Learning Bank to all students over eighteen, regardless of their age or the level of the course.*

- *Educational technology will help to make possible the massive educational expansion, at less than proportional extra cost. The University of Industry will be a key organisation for developing and distributing sub-degree level courses to the expanded student body – be they studying in college, workplace or home.*

- *Sixth-form education should be less specialised. As a first step university entrants should be expected to have at least one A/S level pass in maths, and at least one in an arts or social science subject.*

4

From Welfare to Work

There is no great mystery about why unemployment happens or how to reduce it. The only mystery is why an avoidable misery has proved so politically tolerable.
The Economist, 28 September 1991

WHEN IN 1942 Beveridge listed the five giants which threatened the good society, he named Idleness, Want, Ignorance, Squalor and Disease. Idleness and Want remain undefeated. Unemployment is higher now than it has been for most of the last half-century, and so is the inequality of incomes.

These problems are closely intertwined. For most poor people are not in paid work (see Table 6): they are either unemployed or not working because they are elderly, or sick, or single parents. The elderly are a separate issue, and we leave them to the next chapter. But, for most of the others, the way to a better life is to work and earn. Work will give them the sense of making a contribution, and earnings will provide a better income than benefits ever could. So the basic strategy for dealing with want is to get people from welfare into work.

Table 6: Who are the poor?

	Percentage	
	Poorest 10%	Poorest 20%
No paid work		
Unemployed	26	18
Over 60	25	30
Sick or disabled	10	7
Single mother	10	15
In paid work	29	30
All	100	100

UNEMPLOYMENT

The top priority is to reduce unemployment. In early 1997, nearly 8% of the workforce are without jobs.[1] And over 3% have been out of work for over a year (or over six months if under twenty-five) – the long-term unemployed.

This unemployment is a tragic waste of people's lives. The misery of the unemployed far exceeds the simple loss of income. And society as a whole loses from the waste of precious human potential. Those in work face higher taxes in order to pay for the massive drain in unemployment benefits and lost tax revenue.[2]

If we had no unemployment (an extreme assumption), the Exchequer would be better off by nearly £20 billion a year, through saving on unemployment benefits and collecting more taxes. So unemployment 'costs' each income-tax payer something like £1,000 a year. For the sake of the unemployed and of the taxpayer, something serious has to be done. But can we reduce unemployment without simply pushing up inflation?

The answer is yes, especially if we focus on eliminating

long-term unemployment. Once people have been unemployed that long, their chances of finding work have been largely destroyed (see Figure 12). The very fact of failure makes failure more likely, and many employers will not even look at someone who has been out of work for a long time. This causes despair to the unemployed, but it also tells us exactly what to do: we must re-integrate the long-term unemployed into the workforce. 'Inclusion' must be the guiding principle.

This will not cause extra inflation for one simple reason: employers only give extra wage increases when they experience some new difficulty in recruitment. But since they are already loath to recruit long-term unemployed people, they will not notice if there are fewer of them in the market.[3] So we can reduce unemployment without extra inflation – if we do it by preventing long-term unemployment.[4]

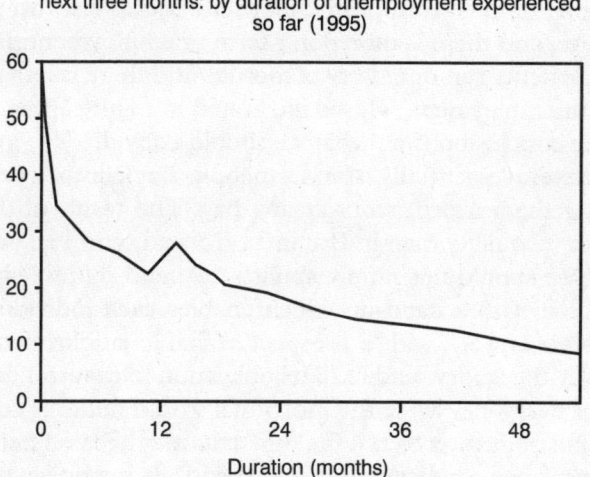

Figure 12: The long-term unemployed have less of a chance

Preventing long-term unemployment

But how? We have to change the way in which unemployed people are treated. Human dignity requires that people gain their income through work rather than hand-outs: work makes people feel useful and needed. So, after a period of unemployment, the state should offer its help not in the form of hand-outs but through the guarantee of work.

This is no airy-fairy idea. It has been the system in Sweden for forty years and is now being implemented in Switzerland and Denmark. The OECD itself has for some time been pushing for a more active approach to unemployment, rather than the passive approach of paying out money.[5]

This shift of emphasis is based in part on the accumulating evidence about what actually causes unemployment.[6] One of the factors which clearly matter is how unemployed people are treated. Where people are offered income for an indefinite period if out of work, people remain unemployed longer. For example, in most European countries benefits last two years or more, and there is more long-term unemployment. In the USA benefits run out after six months and there is less long-term unemployment. This is illustrated in Figure 13.

The conclusion is not that we should copy the US, for the US system essentially starves people back into work by making them accept work at any pay. The result of this is greater inequality than in Britain and a semi-criminal underclass. We should not simply abolish the hand-out; we should replace it with a hand-up which enables each individual to find serious work with a prospect of stable employment. In this way the state would fulfil its obligation to ensure a decent life for everyone, while the individual would fulfil his corresponding obligation to use the opportunities he is offered.

This is not a policy of 'tax and spend'. It is a policy to use better the billions we now waste on benefits paid for doing nothing, in order to help people function as creative members of society. So here is a realistic and costed proposal, which has

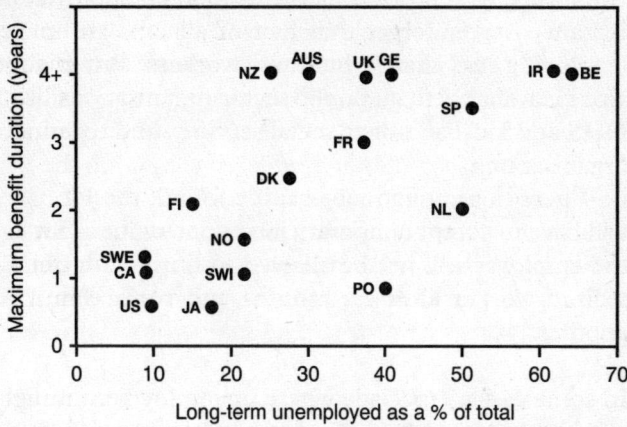

Figure 13: **Long-term benefits lead to long-term unemployment**

been subjected to widespread discussion among employers and others.[7]

- Once people have been unemployed for a year (or six months if under twenty-five), the Employment Service will be obliged to find them at least two offers of reasonable full-time work. These jobs will last at least six months. As now, if people reject job offers they can no longer claim benefit: that is the position now and it would continue to be so.

- The jobs will, wherever possible, be regular jobs with regular employers, paying at least the minimum wage.[8] The inducement to the employer will be that anyone hiring a long-term unemployed person will get a recruitment rebate of £75 a week for six months (£60 a week if the person is under twenty-five). Needless to say, no employer will get the rebate if at the same time he is dismissing workers. The rebate will be particularly attractive to small employers, who provide a large fraction of employment in Britain – never forget that half of all jobs are in firms employing less than a hundred workers. But it should also be available to all public sector organisations like the NHS and local authority social services, and to voluntary organisations.

Where not enough jobs can be found, the Job Centre will have to accept temporary job opportunities. But again the employer will not be allowed to finish with one subsidised worker after six months and replace him with another.

- In some cases, especially where unemployment is high, it may be impossible to find enough jobs with regular employers. In such cases temporary jobs will be provided through job-creation projects run by public authorities or voluntary bodies. There is socially useful work crying out to be done – refurbishing buildings and the environment, improving social services and so on, and many of the unemployed are well suited to this work.[9]

    There are two problems with this type of solution. The work is explicitly temporary, so the worker has to find another job when it ends. This should be helped by the experience the person has gained and the reference that can be provided for him, but even so, it is tough to have to start looking again. The other problem is cost. If the government alone is paying for the work, it will be very expensive if the worker gets a regular full-time wage, and a solution involving benefit plus – where the worker receives unemployment benefit plus £20 a week – may be inevitable.[10] The alternative would be part-time work paid at the rate for the job and topped up where necessary by Family Credit.

- What about training? There are two points here. First,

world-wide experience with training programmes for unemployed people is disappointing (Fay, 1996). What unemployed people want is work, and too often training only leaves people in much the same position as before. The truth is that off-the-job training for unemployed people is very difficult to organise effectively. In general the best policy is to get people into jobs where the employer has his own incentive to do the training.

There are two main exceptions. If a person has a clear picture of what he needs to learn (and is long-term unemployed), he should be able to study full-time for up to six months on benefit plus for a nationally recognised vocational qualification at sub-degree level. Equally, if a person is under twenty-five and does not even have a Level 2 qualification, the employer should be obliged to release the person for one-day-a-week off-the-job education for Level 2.

- These three main alternatives – the recruitment rebate, the job-creation project and education – should encompass a suitable solution for every long-term unemployed person. But to match the opening to the individual is a huge task, and must be the responsibility of the Job Centres. Each unemployed person should have an individual case-worker whose responsibility it is to find a suitable solution for every person on their case-load. From the sixth month onward, the case-worker and the claimant should grapple with possible solutions every time the person signs on, and it should be understood that being unemployed is itself a job – the job being to find work. If work is not available locally, the Job Centre should have funds to finance travel costs to where the work is. The aim is to widen the claimant's range of search, so that employment can expand without running into inflationary bottlenecks.

Thus the Job Centre has to be the key instrument for

making the policy succeed. All the money spent on rebates, job-creation or education should be routed through the Job Centre, since there is no other way it can discharge its duty. And its duty must be quite simple: to find a solution for every long-term unemployed person.

- What is being proposed is a completely new regime. It cannot be introduced overnight. It must be introduced in stages, making sure it succeeds at each step. Young people are the most in need and they may also be the easiest to help. So we should start with the under twenty-fives. By January 1998 we could stop any of them entering long-term unemployment. A year later a similar guarantee should be offered to those aged 25–34 and so on, so that within five years there would be no more long-term unemployed.[11]

EVALUATION

Is it really that easy? It certainly is not easy, but it would work. For much of the pessimism about such schemes is based on a simple misunderstanding. Surely, people say, if employers hire more long-term unemployed people because of a rebate, there are 'others' they would have hired who become unemployed. Total unemployment is unaffected.

This argument overlooks the key point that *the 'others' would have been hired* in the first place. They are not people on whom employers have turned their backs. If one employer does not hire them, another will recognise them as attractive propositions, and will therefore consider that the effective supply of labour which he faces has improved when these people now come knocking at his door. Inflationary pressure will therefore be less than otherwise and the total number of jobs in the economy will expand.[12]

The pessimistic view is based on the alternative theory that there is a job-fund: a fixed amount of work to be done. If this were so, every increase in the labour force would cause an increase in unemployment, and every decrease in the labour force a decrease. There is absolutely no evidence in favour of this view of the world. On the contrary, when countries experience immigration or a 'natural' increase of population, the number of jobs expands and vice versa.[13] If we re-integrate the long-term unemployed and thus expand the supply of attractive labour, we shall increase the total number of jobs.

This is part of the natural adjustment of the labour market. Most people understand that if a factory in London closes, releasing 1,000 workers, there is not a permanent increase in unemployment of 1,000 workers. But, when they discuss recruitment rebates, they regularly argue that, if 1,000 'other' workers are not hired, this 'substitution and displacement' of 1,000 people should be counted as a permanent offset against the benefits of the rebate. There is no scientific basis for this argument. The labour market will, after a while, adjust to absorb them.

So what are the benefits and costs of our proposals? The social benefits are huge. After the twelfth (or sixth) month everyone is doing something productive for at least six months, and thereafter many more will remain in work than would otherwise have been employed at that stage. Of course not all will remain employed, but at a minimum these proposals will reduce unemployment by 400,000. The social cost is minimal – an increase of perhaps 3,000 in the staff of the Job Centres.

From the Exchequer's point of view the balance is of course more even. For much of what it saves on benefit, it spends on rebates and programmes. Some of the rebates are indeed 'deadweight' – money paid out even though the person would have found work anyway – but on the other hand the new policy will prevent substantial fraud. It will in fact do exactly what any good policy should do – provide real active help to those who need help, and remove financial help from those who are abusing it.

I estimate that by the end of a Parliament the scheme could more or less pay for itself, year by year. But while it is building up there is quite a cost to the Exchequer, because the expenditure has to go up first and some of the savings in lower unemployment come later.[14] Altogether the net cost in the first four years would average £0.7 billion a year – well covered by the proceeds of a £3 billion once-for-all Windfall Tax on utilities.

POVERTY IN WORK

If our central objective is for people to find work, the next question is what income they will get if they do so. Unless people can get significantly more in work than when unemployed, the back to work programme will do little to alleviate Want. And many of these low earners will be so disillusioned by work that they alternate endlessly between work and unemployment.[15]

This problem has become more severe because earnings have become increasingly unequal. The spreading out of earnings has many causes – a greater premium on skill, and increased inequality within skill groups as trade union norms are broken and pay becomes increasingly individualised.[16] The result has been that the real hourly earnings of the bottom 10% of workers have risen by only 14% since 1979 – a very small improvement.

To make working more attractive, there are two possible approaches. One is to hold down benefit. This the Conservative government has done, by indexing unemployment benefits to prices rather than earnings (from 1981 onwards). But the other is to raise the income of people in work.

So what can be done to raise the incomes of poor working families? The main thing is to raise skill levels. But there are two other ways as well. The first is to top up people's wages with in-work benefits, and the second is to raise the minimum wage itself.

IN-WORK BENEFITS

The main in-work benefits are Housing Benefit, Council Tax Benefit and (for families with children) Family Credit. All these benefits are income-related and fall as your income rises. If you are unemployed, you already get Housing Benefit and Council Tax Benefit on top of your Job Seeker's Allowance. It follows that if you move into work, you are better off if your net earnings are more than the basic Job Seeker's Allowance – i.e., over £47.90 for a single person over twenty-five or £118.65 if you are married with two young children.[17] The problem is that, if you have children, your earnings may well not meet that test.

That is one reason why Family Credit exists. It guarantees that most families with children will be better off in work than out of work.[18] For some people, however, the difference is quite small. For example, the government calculate for each working family what their income would be out of work. This is then compared with their actual income in work. The ratio of out-of-work to in-work income is shown in Table 7. Half a million families would lose less than 30% of their income by ceasing to work, but all the rest would lose more than that. So the 'unemployment trap', as it is often called, covers fewer people than is often thought. But for these people it is a real problem.

Moreover there are major hassles involved in moving from in-work to out-of-work benefits and vice versa, which act as a

Table 7: For some people it barely pays to work

Number of families for whom income if unemployed equals	
over 90% of income in work	35,000
over 80% of income in work	165,000
over 70% of income in work	510,000

deterrent to taking work. If you take a job after over six months out of work, you are guaranteed that your Housing Benefit will be paid at the old rate for at least four weeks. But your Family Credit may take a long time to come through. It should be the task of the Job Centre to get the Family Credit for you, and to pay the Job Seeker's Allowance until the Family Credit comes through.

More important, people worry about taking work because of the difficulty of getting back on to benefits quickly if the job falls through or turns out to be no good. This fear has increased as more and more jobs have become insecure and job turnover has gone up in what is an increasingly dynamic labour market. Again, rapid processing is critical, and more people should have a simple right to resume their previous benefit immediately if they become unemployed again within two months.[19]

A big problem with the earnings-related benefits is the 'poverty' trap. Since the benefits are there to reduce poverty, they have to be less for people on higher incomes. Unless the rate at which benefits are withdrawn as income rises is quite high, we should be giving benefits to half the families in the country. So most people on these benefits face quite high 'withdrawal' rates or 'effective marginal tax rates': their total income rises very slowly as their earnings rise.[20] As Table 8 shows, roughly 600,000 families face withdrawal rates of over 70%: from each extra pound they earn they benefit by under

Table 8: Many poor people face high 'effective marginal tax rates'

Families with 'effective marginal tax rates'	Number
over 90%	100,000
over 80%	420,000
over 70%	615,000
over 50%	630,000

30 pence. We must do something to reduce these withdrawal rates in order to improve incentives to take a better paid job or work longer hours.[21]

That is one priority. But 75% of couples on Family Credit leave it within half a year – generally by increasing their income. So at least as high a priority is to raise the level of Family Credit at the bottom end – for the poorest families. This is needed as a matter of justice and as an incentive to work rather than remain unemployed. And, to encourage both spouses to work, the supplement to a given income should be higher if both spouses are working. Perhaps the most important objective of all is to improve take-up, which is now only 70–80% for Family Credit.[22] If a company employs someone on a weekly wage which could make them eligible for Family Credit, it should be obliged to put the relevant claim form in their pay packet.[23]

Another proposal is to extend the coverage of the top-up principle to include people without children. The government is currently piloting an Earnings Top-Up, which would work in a similar way to Family Credit, but for single people and for couples without children. But these groups already receive Housing and Council Tax Benefits, and a further extension does not seem a top priority, for many reasons. The government has a far greater duty to protect children than adults; the unemployment trap is much more extreme for parents than for people without children; and a system of universal top-up would be an invitation to employers to cut wages further.

MINIMUM WAGES

This brings us to the second way in which the government can help to prevent poverty at work. From 1909 until 1993 Britain had, like almost every civilised country, a system of statutory minimum wages. In 1909 Winston Churchill introduced the Trades Boards, which eventually evolved into the Wages

Councils and covered almost all parts of the economy where pay was low.[24] However, the Conservative government argued that employment could be increased if pay was allowed to fall, and the Wages Councils were abolished in 1993.[25]

Since then the lowest wages in these sectors have fallen substantially, but there are no signs that employment has responded. Indeed, over the whole history of the Wages Councils it is difficult to detect any clear evidence that their wage settlements affected employment in their sectors.[26] The reason for this is probably that low-paid labour is very immobile. This gives local employers substantial power in the labour market, and they are often able to pay their workers less than the value of what the workers contribute. So, at this low level of pay, a smallish pay rise may not reduce employment. In some cases it can even increase it, by providing a greater incentive to work (and to work hard).

In the US too, changes in the minimum wage have no clearly visible effect on the number of jobs. This is probably because, as with the old Wages Councils, the number of people whose pay was pushed up by the Minimum Wage is fairly limited – some 5% after the increase of 1991. Where the minimum wage is much higher, as in France, it is far more likely to affect employment. For example, in France the minimum wage affects some 11% of workers and is probably one reason for France's unemployment problem.[27]

There are three powerful arguments for having a minimum wage. First, it prevents the sense of unfairness which goes with excessively low pay. Second, people rightly prefer to earn their income rather than having it topped up by a hand-out. Third, a minimum wage protects the state against the risk that employers will deliberately cut wages, knowing that the state will pick up the difference. This was what happened in the early 1800s under the infamous Speenhamland System, and there are signs that it is starting up again in Britain as a result of our present in-work benefits. Just as landlords abuse Housing Benefit, so employers may abuse the benefit system.[28]

A minimum wage cannot on its own abolish poverty in work. For the majority of those who benefit are either working wives or children living at home – and most of their families are outside the bottom fifth of working families in terms of income per head – because they have at least two earners. In the poorest working families the key determinants of income will always be the level of in-work benefits. But the minimum wage has some role to play in fighting poverty. Given this and the previous arguments, we ought in Britain to revert to a system of minimum wages.

A Labour government would introduce a national minimum wage, whose level will be fixed after recommendations from a new Low Pay Commission. Clearly the wage must be high enough to make a serious difference to a good number of people. But it must be low enough to avoid the direct pricing of people out of jobs, and to limit inflationary pressure as other workers above the minimum try to restore their differentials.[29]

In thinking about how to set the minimum, one approach is to see how many people different levels of the minimum would affect. This is shown in Table 9. Even if people under twenty-one were exempt, a minimum wage of £3.25 an hour would affect 6% of workers – more than the proportion affected in many other European countries (see Table 10). If such a minimum was extended to those aged 18–21, it would affect a quarter of that age group.

Another approach is to say, 'Let's go back to what we would have had with the Wages Councils, since that system worked reasonably well.' If we update the average of the minima established by the Wages Councils in 1993, we get a figure of £3.30. Yet another approach is to look at the distribution of wages of people entering employment from non-employment. A quarter of these 'entry' jobs are paid less than £3.30 an hour (and a half less than £4.30).[30] We should certainly worry about the danger of closing off too many of these opportunities.

So those who fix the minimum wage will need to balance

Table 9: Low pay

Percentage with hourly wages under	Workers aged 21–65 (60 for women)	Workers aged 18–21
£3.00	5	21
£3.25	6	24
£3.50	9	34
£3.75	12	42
£4.00	15	52
£4.25	19	56

Table 10: Minimum wages in other countries

	Percentage of workers at minimum or close to it	Lower minimum wage exists for workers aged under
Austria	4	–
Belgium	4	23
Denmark	6	18
France	11	18 (or trainees)
Luxembourg	11	21
Netherlands	3	22
Portugal	8	18
Spain	7	18
Sweden	0	24
USA	5	21

ambition with discretion. The minimum cannot simply ratify the actual, and there are various measures which can work with a minimum wage to make the whole project workable. First, we must have recruitment subsidies to offset the cost of employing the long-term unemployed. Second, we can use the savings from the higher tax receipts to reduce the employers' National Insurance contributions for low-paid workers (and eliminate the discontinuous jumps in the scale which encourage employers to reduce hours of work in order to save tax). Finally, and in the long-run most important, we must upgrade the skills of the lowest paid in order to justify their higher pay. In 1867 the wider suffrage increased the pressure for better education; so now higher pay should be a source of increased pressure for better skills.

MOTHERS AND CHILDREN

But many of the poorest people in the country are neither unemployed nor working (see Table 11). They are simply living on benefit at a miserable standard of living. For example, 1.2 million single mothers are neither working nor looking for work, but live on Income Support, together with their 2 million children.

The position of the children is the most tragic of all. Altogether, one in three of our children is living on benefits – a truly desperate situation. Income Support pays only £16.45 a week per child (£24.10 if over the age of eleven).[31] For most of us, it is almost impossible to imagine what kind of life can be lived on such an income.

Table 11: People under 60 living on main means-tested benefits (thousands)

	Adults	*Children*
In work	906	1,180
Unemployed	2,288	796
Out of the labour force	2,333	2,347
Total	5,527	4,323
(Total population)	(35,603)	(11,402)

What Labour Can Do

This shocking situation requires a fundamental rethink of our strategy towards family poverty. In general the best way to help poor children is to help their mothers go out to work and earn. Many mothers would like to do this, but they find it too difficult or expensive to arrange the child-care. To change this requires a many-faceted attack:

- Nursery education must be available for all three- and four-year-olds (on a contribution basis). It should be full-time or part-time, as desired.

- For children of regular school age, supervised activities must be available outside school hours and during school holidays and half-terms. (Even 'Baker Days', when the staff all go for training, cause enormous difficulty for working mothers.) Many children would gain enormously from supervised activities, including supervised homework. In many homes it is difficult to work quietly, and much easier to get your homework done if you do it before getting caught up at home in television and housework. Imaginative proposals for developing out-of-school activities are now being piloted. Parents who can afford to pay should make a contribution, and the residual cost of the activities could easily pay for itself in benefit and tax savings – and in lives enriched.

- When the children are young, it is reasonable that mothers should have a choice about whether to seek work. But there is a real question of whether, in today's world, mothers of older children who ask for Income Support should not be expected to look for work – as happens in France. This issue arises both for lone mothers and for wives of unemployed men.

- A policy of active help will require a quite new type of Employment Service, which provides counselling, Job

Clubs and job placement – not just to unemployed claimants but to anybody wanting to get back to work.

LONG-TERM SICK

One group who particularly need help are the long-term sick on Incapacity Benefit. Nearly two million families of working age now get this benefit, half as many again as five years ago. As with unemployment, the increase is not because the number coming on to benefit is rising, but because people are staying on the benefit for longer. Many would be better off if they were helped back to work. To encourage this, the recruitment subsidy for the long-term unemployed should also be available if an employer hires someone off Incapacity Benefit.[32]

The problem with incapacity is that a person is often incapacitated for some types of work but not for others. Doctors cannot be expected to know what types of work are available, and they naturally agree that someone who can no longer do their former work is unable to work in general. To help the claimant explore the actual opportunities which exist, it would be a real help if a member of the Employment Service could join the doctors who assess whether the claimant could in fact hope to work again.

REMEDIES OF LIMITED USE

Is there anything else we can do to promote employment? The consensus of mainstream research is that three main factors matter: the treatment of unemployed people, the level of skills and the system of wage determination. But many other remedies have been proposed: regional policy, lower National Insurance taxes, work-sharing, early retirement and further deregulation of the labour market. There is no clear evidence that any of these would have a major effect on unemployment.[33] But we ought, nevertheless, to consider their pros and cons.

- **Regional policy** can certainly do something, especially when it improves road access and communications. But regional aid through industrial subsidies tends to go to large firms who are better at lobbying than providing jobs to people who are hard to place in work. If we go back to fundamentals, the argument for regional policy is that some regions have more unemployed people than others. So the most obvious regional policy is simply to help the unemployed wherever they may be, as we have proposed. Regions where there are more unemployed people will then get more help than others, but the help will be targeted where it is needed. In practice, so-called regional unemployment is highly concentrated within particular localities within a region. Many estates desperately need help of all kinds, and local economic initiatives are enormously important. But they need to originate within the region, not in Whitehall.

- Some people argue that employers' **National Insurance contributions** are killing jobs, because they are quite simply a 'tax on jobs'. This view has been pushed by the European Commission (1993), who suggested that jobs would expand if taxes on employers were reduced and taxes on goods increased. There is no convincing evidence in favour of this belief.[34] Of course taxes can produce inflationary pressures by robbing workers of the fruits of their labour, and this pressure can translate into job losses. But this is true of all taxes, not just those on employers. And the extra unemployment can only be temporary – otherwise unemployment today would now be many times what it was in the nineteenth century, when taxes were so much lower.

- Another remedy proposed by some European leaders, like Jacques Delors, is **work-sharing**. Of course, in a temporary downturn it makes no sense for a company to lay off workers who will eventually be needed again – better to share out the existing work. And in the longer term there is a downward trend in hours of work all over the world – which reflects the fact that, as people get richer, they choose to work less. The illusion is to push things faster than this (by legislation or by subsidy), and to suppose that you can thereby get a permanent increase in the number of jobs.

What will happen is this. At first the number of jobs will expand, but then companies will find labour in short supply and inflationary pressure will develop. The monetary authorities will then act to restrain inflation, and unemployment will rise back to the level at which inflation is under control. Thus we shall end up with the same number of people in work, but with each of them working shorter hours and producing less. In other words we shall be poorer. There is good evidence that this is what happens.[35]

- The same logic applies to **early retirement**. If the government persuades people to retire earlier, this will reduce the supply of labour and increase inflationary pressure. The monetary authorities will act to correct this, and we shall end up with the same unemployment rate. But the labour force is now smaller, so that fewer people are in work. Once again we are poorer. This is hardly what we want, especially at a time when the number of people of working age is rising slowly compared with the number of elderly people they have to support. For the state to add artificially to the number of dependants would be the height of folly. Quite different of course is the position of companies. If they have to contract, a humane policy of voluntary retirement may well be the best way. But the state should do all in its power to help these people find other work. Ageism should be a major target for government attack.

- Perhaps the most fashionable nostrum for cutting unemployment is **a more flexible labour market**. This is certainly the view of the current British government, who (in league with the Americans) have persuaded the OECD to publicise the idea.[36] Europe, they say, is suffering from a sclerosis of over-regulation. This includes excessive minimum wages in some countries (which I have already noted), but it also includes limits on the rights of companies to fire their workers. In Britain these limits have already been eliminated for workers employed for under two years. But should they be reduced further?

  There is no clear evidence that employment protection increases unemployment overall. On the one hand it discourages companies from taking on workers, because they are then difficult to fire; this increases long-term unemployment. But on the other hand it directly reduces firing, and so reduces short-term unemployment. On balance there seems to be no clear effect on overall unemployment, one way or the other.[37] But older workers gain and younger ones lose.

  For these reasons excessive employment protection is a bad idea. But there is no reason why we in Britain should go any further down that road. A high-turnover economy has many drawbacks – above all that employers have less incentive to invest in their workers.

  So what should we think about the European Social Chapter, which could lead to further regulation of the British labour market? The argument for a European element in social policy is of course that countries may obtain unfair competitive advantage by providing bad working conditions. In itself the argument is not very strong, since wages and the right to strike are carefully excluded from any form of European Union interference – and it is not clear why other features of the employment contract should be included. However, that is how our European partners have chosen to proceed. If we want to be full members of Europe we should join in, unless the risks are too great.

So what are the risks? Under the Social Chapter unanimity is required on issues of employee representation, protection from dismissal and social security. So we face no risk of being overruled on those issues. But, for some other subjects, rules can be established by qualified majority voting. These subjects are health and safety, working conditions, information for and consultation of workers, gender equality, and the integration of people excluded from the labour market. We could probably live with these also. So far only two rules have been established – giving fathers rights of leave on the birth of a child, and requiring 'European works councils' in companies with significant operations in more than one country. The threats arising from the Social Chapter have been greatly exaggerated. If we want to be full members of the European Union, we should join quickly and thus have the ability to influence what happens.

CONCLUSION

The welfare-to-work strategy must be the centrepiece of any attack on poverty. It will not only raise incomes while people are of working age. It will also help to raise their pension contributions, so that they can have a decent old age. But pensions are a matter for the next chapter.

Summary

- *We should prevent people entering long-term unemployment. Employers are not keen to recruit people who have been unemployed for a long time. So long-term unemployment can be abolished without increasing the shortage of labour – and thus without increasing inflation.*

- *Everyone still unemployed after a year (or six months if under twenty-five) should be guaranteed offers of work lasting at least six months. As now, people refusing offers would lose their benefits.*

- *Job offers would be secured by using the money which would have been wasted on benefits. Regular employers, public, private or voluntary, would be offered £75 a week for six months for hiring a long-term unemployed person (£60 if under twenty-five). The job would be full-time and the wage at least the Minimum Wage. Where not enough jobs can be found this way, job-creation projects should be introduced which could provide temporary work for six months.*

- *In-work benefits have a key role in preventing poverty and increasing the reward for working. But benefit procedures should make it much easier to move directly from unemployment benefits to in-work benefits (and vice versa), without a hiatus when no money is coming in. It is the fear of this hiatus which discourages so many unemployed people from taking work.*

- *To make sure that low earners get their in-work benefits, employers should automatically enclose the relevant forms in the pay packet of any worker who might be eligible. If possible, the level of Family Credit should also be raised.*

- *There should be a Minimum Wage designed to raise the wage of a significant number of people but not so many as to jeopardise employment. A minimum wage which covered 10% of workers, as in France, would probably be too high. There are strong arguments for excluding from the regulations people under twenty-one, most of whom should be trainees.*

- *To help more mothers to work, there should be universal availability of nursery education from the age of three and of supervised out-of-school activities after school and during school holidays. Parents who can afford to do so should make a contribution. Where adequate out-of-school facilities are available, mothers of school-age children could be expected to look for work if they wished to draw benefit.*

- *More effort should be made to find suitable work for people who are now unable, for health reasons, to do their traditional work.*

- *Some of the proposed remedies for joblessness would be unlikely to succeed – including lower average 'taxes on jobs', shorter working hours, earlier retirement, and further deregulation of the labour market (i.e. reduced employment protection).*

- *If we want to be full partners in Europe, we should sign the Social Chapter. The risks to employment are small.*

5

The Proper Size of Government

It is very easy to accuse a government of imperfection, for all mortal things are full of it.

Montaigne

How high should taxes be? Or equivalently, since taxes pay for government, what size of government do we want?[1] The Conservative Party has pledged itself to cut government expenditure to below 40% of our national income, and Mr Major is thought to favour a goal of under 35%. Does this make sense? Or is the current size of government all right – or even too small?

INTERNATIONAL COMPARISONS

There are a number of ways to approach the question. One, rather crude, way is to see if we are out of line with other similar countries, and if so whether this has any detectable effect on our rate of economic growth. As Figure 14 shows, Britain has a much smaller government share than most European countries. But should we have still less? Is there any evidence that smaller government increases economic growth?

As a first pass, we can simply take the advanced OECD countries and see whether those with small government are

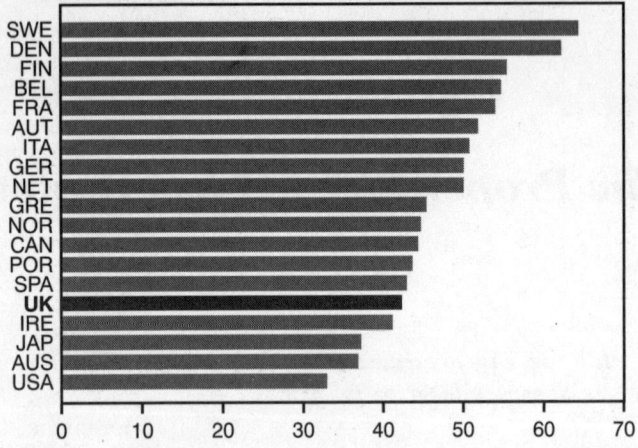

Figure 14: Britain has smaller government than most of Europe

growing faster. This is done in Figure 15; there is no relation. Two main countries have smaller government than us, Japan and the USA; Japan grew faster than us, the USA slower. As regards continental Europe, most of these countries have much larger government than us, but on average they grew at the same rate as we did. So no clear pattern emerges.

But what if we bring in the Far East? Chris Patten has said that they are an object lesson to us, and show that small government is good for growth. These countries do indeed have smaller government than us and have grown faster. But why just bring in the Far East? If we bring in other non-OECD countries, we shall find many countries with small government that have grown very slowly. And so again we are forced into a more careful analysis, where we look simultaneously at all the factors affecting growth.

The conclusion we now reach is that high education and low inequality are both favourable to growth – and these are

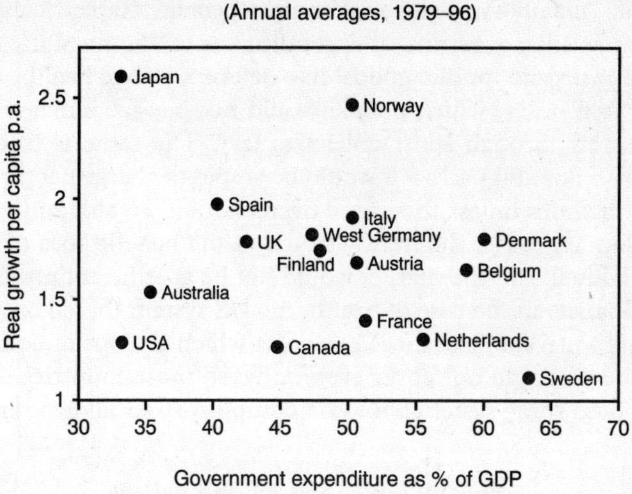

The Proper Size of Government

(Annual averages, 1979–96)

[Scatter plot: Real growth per capita p.a. vs Government expenditure as % of GDP. Data points: Japan (~33, 2.6), Norway (~50, 2.45), Spain (~40, 1.95), Italy (~50, 1.9), West Germany (~48, 1.8), UK (~43, 1.8), Denmark (~60, 1.8), Finland (~47, 1.75), Austria (~51, 1.7), Belgium (~59, 1.65), Australia (~36, 1.55), France (~51, 1.4), USA (~33, 1.3), Netherlands (~55, 1.3), Canada (~45, 1.3), Sweden (~63, 1.1).]

Figure 15: No relation between small government and growth

strikingly present in the Far East. With these features plus strong social discipline and a low initial income, it is not surprising that the Far East has been growing rapidly. Most researchers conclude that the size of government as such has no clear effect on economic growth.[2]

This is hardly surprising given the huge variety of things on which the government spends its money. The only sound approach to the issue is to think about each of these things and to ask whether they are worth the taxes that pay for them. No one should advocate extra spending without saying how it will be paid for – but nor should anyone advocate lower taxes without saying what spending they would cut.

WHAT ARE WE GETTING FOR OUR MONEY?

So what does our money go on? Government spending has two main objectives: to finance services which the market would underprovide, and to transfer money from rich to poor – mainly through social security benefits. Table 12 shows what existing government expenditure is on. Some of the services are pure 'public goods' like defence, public health, and law and order, which people would not pay for individually but only through some collective levy. The same is true of most roads and parks – it would be stupid to charge people for the facilities unless they were overcrowded. Health and education are rather different – much of the benefit goes to the individual. But the market would not be an efficient provider of finance. In the case of health, the US system (based on voluntary private insurance) has costs which are out of control and even so do not cover everybody; so most countries have adopted some system based on compulsory social insurance.

Table 12: Public expenditure 1995–96

			Percentage of GDP
Health			5.6
Education			5.1
Defence			3.0
Law, police, fire services			2.2
Environmental services			1.4
Transport (roads, rail)			1.3
Personal social services			1.3
Housing			0.7
Employment			0.5
Social security:	Elderly	5.5	
	Sick and disabled	3.1	
	Unemployed	1.3	
	Families	2.4	
	Widows and others	0.9	
			13.1
Other			7.9
Total			42.1

The Proper Size of Government

As regards education, children are extremely vulnerable, especially when their parents are poor or ill-educated. Under purely private education, most would get less education than they should (in terms of the overall benefit to themselves and the wider society). And the society would become increasingly divided. So throughout the world most education is financed by the state, which of course gets a good rake-off in higher taxes from the higher income which education produces.

It is remarkable how similar are the levels of expenditure on education and health in most advanced countries (relative to GDP), though Britain spends less on health than most. We would not want to see these services deteriorate. And there is a further point. As people get richer, there are some goods where people are nearing saturation (like food), and desired expenditure grows more slowly than national income. But there are others, including health and education, where desired expenditure rises faster than income.[3] These pressures are exacerbated in the case of health by ageing populations, and in the case of education by rising numbers of children.[4] Such pressures are a major problem. Over the next decade we shall have to find at least another 1–2% of GDP for health and education.

Where can we get it from?[5] Either from higher taxes, or from savings elsewhere in the budget. This directs attention at the growing bill for social security, even though by European standards ours is not huge. Social security performs a key role in redistributing income. This is illustrated in Figure 16, which shows how much different people get from the welfare state (shown in black) and how much they contribute (shaded). The difference is the dotted line. If you are poor, you are a major net beneficiary of the system, and if you are rich you are a major net contributor. If we want a just society, we must have some such system of redistribution.

However, some aspects of the system are more truly redistributive than others. For example, many of the benefits help people at moments when they have low income; and the same

What Labour Can Do

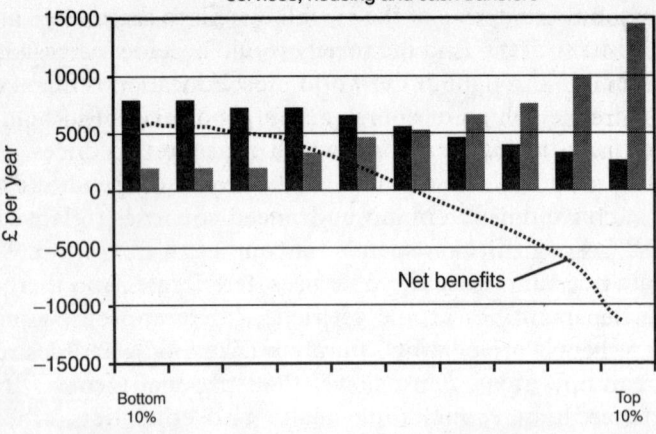

Figure 16: The process of redistribution

people then pay in when they have high income. In these cases the system transfers income between different points in the lifetime of the same individual, rather than transferring between people whose lives have been rich and poor. This is true of, for example, pensions and Child Benefit.[6] To have these transfers done automatically is very convenient, and in the past it has been for many people a matter of life and death. However, economic growth strengthens people's position in life and capital markets are improving, making it easier for people to shift their money around between different periods of life. They borrow when income is low and save when income is high. Thus it becomes reasonable, as time passes, not necessarily to cut this kind of welfare provision but to let some of it grow less fast than the growth of national income.[7] But any such change will surely be offset by growth in other areas like education and health.

WHERE NEXT?

So, when one looks at what public expenditure goes on, there is no obvious reason to reduce its share in national income below 40%. There are of course political pressures which may tend to increase public expenditure for bad reasons. Producer pressure groups come lobbying for subsidies, even though these are contrary to the interests of consumers. Since consumers are not well organised, the lobbyists sometimes prevail; but such subsidies are not now a major feature of the British scene.[8] Again, ministers may be able to improve their reputations by winning money in the Cabinet, rather than by cutting their departmental budgets; but it often goes the other way.

So there is no presumption that political pressures produce excessive public expenditure in Britain,[9] and there is no clear evidence that lower public expenditure would increase economic growth. It would certainly be very difficult to cut the shares of government expenditure substantially. As Table 13 shows, after seventeen years of trying, the Tories had barely reduced the share of public spending below the level they inherited in 1979.[10] To reduce it substantially below 40% would require a major bloodletting.

But why not go above 40%? In principle the figure should not be decided on its own. It should emerge from a scrutiny of each programme and what changes in spending would

Table 13: **The rising bill for social security**
(percentage of GDP)

	Social security	Education	Health and personal social services	Defence	Other	Total
1979–80	9.8	5.1	5.4	4.6	17.6	42.5
1995–96	13.1	5.1	6.9	3.0	14.0	42.1

justify the corresponding changes in taxes. However, this rational procedure is very difficult to apply in practice, and a natural starting point is to ask whether we can achieve our main objectives with the existing level of taxation (relative to national income). For, whatever people say in response to questions about their willingness to pay higher taxes, it certainly appears that, when they go to the ballot box, a key part of the electorate votes against higher taxes.

If we accept this constraint for the moment, we start from a situation where taxes and other receipts amount to 38% of national income. If we want to stop our government debt rising relative to national income, we cannot have an average deficit of more than 2% of national income (see Chapter 7).[11] This would mean that government expenditure must average no more than 40% of national income.

This is a tight constraint. We are starting from a position where expenditure now planned on the present government's policies is likely to be 40% of national income in 1997/8 and falling only slowly thereafter.[12] This means that, unless there are further tax revenues, it would be difficult to initiate new spending early in the next Parliament.[13] That is why Labour proposes an immediate Windfall Tax on the utilities to enable it to attack youth unemployment. But even after 2000 the position will remain tight. There is of course the 'growth dividend': as real income rises, so do tax receipts. So real tax receipts will rise by some $2\frac{1}{2}$% a year over the course of a cycle. But the period 2000–02 may be one of below trend growth and there is always the problem of public sector pay. In recent years the growth in public sector pay has been financed through cuts in staff, but this may not be practicable for much longer.[14]

TAXING ANTI-SOCIAL ACTIVITY

The general prospect is therefore difficult. Budget forecasts alter from month to month – on both the tax and expenditure sides. So it makes no sense to make exact proposals about future taxes, but two things are clear: Labour would like to cut income tax for low earners,[15] and it may have to consider raising other less odious taxes.

The obvious route is to pay for social action through higher taxes on anti-social action. There are many ways in which an extra 1–2% of GDP could be levied through taxes on pollution, alcohol and tobacco.

Most pollution is created by cars and power stations. Driving can be discouraged by taxes on petrol (4p a litre on petrol would raise £1.5 billion) and more could be raised by taxing power station inputs (coal, gas and oil). There is also of course an overwhelming case for road-user charges which charge people for driving down congested streets.[16] But such 'road pricing' would have to be left to local authorities (except perhaps for the M25) and it would in any case take time to introduce.

There is also a strong case for heavier taxes on alcohol.[17] There is a real problem here, arising from the steady increase in real income. As people become richer, they will buy more and more alcohol unless its relative price rises. This will increase social disturbance and road accidents, and impose costs on the NHS through accidents and illness. Clearly many young people are already drinking more than their bodies can stand.

Smoking too imposes costs on the NHS, and could also be taxed more heavily. If an incoming Labour government had to explain to the people that it had found the public finances in a deplorable state, making social improvements impossible without extra taxes on anti-social activity, the public would surely support this. These taxes would be thoroughly justified on externality grounds.[18] But their incidence is regressive, and there would have to be some offset in lower income taxes on poorer people.

We can now look at the expenditure side. If education and health are to grow faster than income, some items will eventually have to grow slower. So what can grow more slowly? One obvious item is defence. It is not clear that it needs to grow in real terms – except perhaps to meet rising real wage costs. Indeed some existing items are quite questionable: the Eurofighter, for example, will cost Britain £15 billion in order to improve our ability to beat Russia. But defence is a smallish item. The main saving has got to be on social security, which has up to now been growing faster than any other sector (see Table 13).

Benefits to unemployed people can certainly be drastically reduced by active labour market policy (see Chapter 4). But the benefits which unemployed people receive are only about one tenth of the total benefit bill. In time, expenditure on single-parent families and the long-term sick can also be reduced by policies of welfare-to-work. But all these policies will cost the government at least as much as they save on benefit. So how else can we ensure that the social security budget does not get out of control?

PENSIONS

The main focus has to be on pensions. The government's approach has been to index pensions (and other benefits) to prices rather than earnings.[19] The result is that the relative income of pensioners with no private income has fallen drastically. This has been one of the many reasons for the appalling increase in inequality in the last eighteen years.

How can we right this wrong, without yet another surge in public expenditure? The answer requires a two-pronged strategy. The state will have to insist that people make more provision for their own old age, while at the same time providing a better deal for those who for one reason or another fall through the net.

The better deal does not require a rise in the basic pension, which would benefit all pensioners whether they were poor or rich. But it does require that the minimum income for pensioners (provided through Income Support) should rise in line with living standards gradually, and not be stuck for ever where it was in 1981.[20] Only in this way can we hope to prevent the remorseless increase in relative poverty.[21]

But in the longer run it is the second part of the strategy that matters most. Eventually every old person should have a second income based on their own savings, as a supplement to the state pension.[22] This will in fact be a more secure source of income than the promises of governments. Pensioners are relatively poor today because state pensions stopped rising in line with earnings, as people had expected. This shows the dangers of a system of income support which relies too heavily on the government of the day. The same trickery has been practised over the SERPS – the State Earnings Related Pension Scheme. This was agreed on a bipartisan basis in 1975, with specified contributions and benefits. Since then the promised benefits have twice been cut in half.

Thus the best way forward is that individuals should increasingly have to save for a private second-tier pension that is 'theirs'. SERPS would be gradually phased out. Under the new scheme the state would lay down minimum levels of contribution and would also specify minimum standards for insurance company schemes. These standards would include reasonable economy of administration, as occurs in occupational pensions but not in highly personalised pension plans. The changeover from SERPS to an individual pension would of course have to be gradual.

A scheme of this kind could also have a major effect on our national rate of saving and investment.[23] For one problem with our present pension system is that it is a Pay-As-You-Go system, under which current workers pay the pensions of those no longer working. In this process no money is saved and invested, in order to provide a future return from which the pension can be paid. Asian Tiger countries have gained from not having Pay-As-You-Go pensions, so that workers have saved a much higher fraction of their income to provide for old age. Sometimes the saving has been compulsory (as with the Singapore National Provident Fund) and sometimes voluntary. We should bring in a compulsory requirement that people save a certain proportion of their income in a second-tier private pension.

There are of course major problems with any new approach – in particular the problem of people who, due to low earnings, unemployment or family responsibilities, have low or non-existent earnings from which to save. For such people the state would have to make appropriate contributions. Provided this is done, we would have in place a pension system which is better than any likely system financed by higher taxes, for two reasons. People could be sure of a decent income in old age, and we should have higher economic growth.

Of course this change has a cost. People will have more deductions on their pay slip. But voting behaviour clearly suggests that people are more willing to pay for a pension that is theirs than they are to pay into a National Insurance Fund which is anything but funded and pays benefits to different people from those who are contributing. We already have a more developed private pension system than most countries – with two-thirds of current pensioners receiving an occupational pension worth on average over £70 a week.[24] The natural way forward is to expand and universalise it. In this way everybody will have a stake in their own pension.

Old age has a second problem, beyond the general need for income. Over two million old people need long-term care in a residential home or as invalids living at home. The total cost of this is already around 1.8% of national income, and it will grow.[25] Under the present system, this care is publicly available on an undignified means-tested basis, which often destroys the ability of parents to leave their homes to their children because the home has to be sold to pay for care. This situation calls for an insurance solution.

The need for long-term care is something which could

befall anyone. It is not like ill-health, where some people are much more at risk than others. It is therefore easier to handle through market or semi-market methods. Each person should be contributing to an old-age care insurance which would be triggered if they became in need of care. In order to increase the stakeholder element, it is important that individuals feel they have their own policies, and people who contributed more got a better quality of environment – though not of publicly-provided medical care.

PRIVATE FINANCE INITIATIVE

The merit of these two proposals is that they will both improve the lives of the elderly, while at the same time allowing for the improvements in health care and education that people want. Another device adopted by the present government looks as if it does the same, but it has serious problems. This is the so-called Private Finance Initiative, under which private firms are encouraged to undertake public sector projects using private money for the up-front investment, and then being paid in return an annual rent or service charge. The scheme has been slow to get started, due to the inevitable red tape, and the biggest projects agreed so far have been transport projects (for the London Docklands Light Railway, London's Northern Line Underground and Scotland's Air Traffic Control). But the government's hope is to extend the idea widely into hospitals, prisons and the like, including a major element of private management.

How far should this process go? That depends on two questions. First, does this really enable more of the projects that should be undertaken to get done? There is a problem here. For private operators who borrow money pay much higher interest rates than the government – because the government debt is 'as safe as houses', or more so. So private operators will charge a higher rent than the interest payments which government-financed projects would have to pay –

unless the private provider is a lot more efficient than the public provider would have been. So in many cases the PFI will cost the government more in the end than if it had done the thing itself.

But then we bump up against the arbitrary limits on the level of government expenditure. If the government would not in fact have financed the project because of these limits, it may be better to have the project privately financed than not done at all. But it might be even better to make the limits less arbitrary. If the private sector builds something and rents it to the government, the government still has to pay. It just pays later. It is a form of trickery to pretend that because the expenditure is outside *today's* PSBR it is off the PSBR altogether – unless it is a project for which the public eventually pays in charges (rail fares or the like). Otherwise, if it is a prison or a hospital, it will eventually come out of the PSBR – but later. Eventually the taxpayer pays, so why fool people?[26]

The only sensible reason for having a PFI is when the private sector can do the job better. There may be many cases where this is so in the transport field, including possibly some toll-roads as on the Continent. The private sector may also have a role as builders of hospitals or prisons. But they should surely not be given long-term contracts to provide clinical services, for the set of tasks to be done may easily change, and the contractual relationship introduces an unnecessary rigidity into the situation.

Contracts and public service

This raises the general issue of the use of contracts and tendering in the provision of public services. These have been steadily increasing, from the contracting out of dust-collection (one of the first) to the contracting out of prisons and the Careers Service. There has also been a major revolution inside the National Health Service, with the introduction of the internal market, where purchasers (GPs and local health authorities) contract with providers (like hospitals).

The arguments for these changes are clear. They force costs out into the open – since price affects who gets the tender. And, supposedly, they put the interests of the consumer of the services into the driving seat.

The problems are equally clear. There is an immense increase in paperwork. More important, the judgment of the conscientious professional is now replaced by financial incentives and rules, which undermine the commitment and dedication of the professional and may often lead to worse rather than better decisions. And of course there is the very rigidity of the contracts, as exemplified by the case of Nicholas Geldard, who may have died because the scanner at the Stepping Hill hospital no longer belonged to the hospital but was contracted to it for a limited number of hours a day. When everything is in contracts, people who used to help each other out as a matter of comradely behaviour are less inclined to do so.

There is also loss of collective memory. When work is done within an organisation, people remember what has been tried and what has succeeded. But when the work is doled out on fixed-term-contracts, there is a danger of re-inventing the wheel. And even the identity of the activity becomes obscure: who now can *find* the Careers Service?

Finally, the subtlety of the true objectives of an activity can easily get diluted in favour of a limited set of performance targets which can be written down in contracts. Similar problems of specification of course arise within any large firm, and the main reason why large firms exist rather than hundreds of sub-contractors is the difficulty of foreseeing all eventualities and writing them down in contract form. Instead people are employed who can respond to the emerging situation either by being told what to do or by the use of their own professional intelligence, which is what they are employed for.

The contractual model can have a function in clarifying

objectives, but it often reflects the view that people cannot be trusted, even when their promotion prospects depend on good performance. For some time firms, like governments, moved in the direction of more contractual relationships within their organisations: with profit centres paying each other for supplies and services received, and with performance-related pay. But now the tide has begun to turn back – with more trust and more co-operation between departments. It is surely time to slow down the growth of contractual relationships within the public sector.

VOUCHERS

A different method of contracting out is to put power directly into the hands of consumers. Under this regime, it is not the government or the health authority which buys a block of services from a provider: the purchaser is the individual consumer. Thus in education the state would provide every child with a voucher which could be used to buy education in any school. This is the present government's policy for nursery education. But there are a number of problems.

The first key issue is whether the voucher can be topped-up by private money, so that consumers who want to buy a better service can do so by spending more. On the face of it that sounds a great idea – if people are willing to spend more on something, it must surely be efficient to let them do so. This argument may, however, run counter to the reasons why the state was providing money in the first place.

Suppose for example that a major government objective is to raise every child to at least a certain standard by the age of eighteen. If it simply provides £x to every child and lets those who want to pay more, how will the level of x be determined in the political arena? Many voters would be quite keen to let the value of the voucher fall somewhat, because this would cut their taxes, and they could always top the money up for their own child.[27] By contrast, under present arrangements those same voters have a greater incentive to vote for high education expenditure. Today their children are bound to suffer if the basic standard is low (unless they go right outside the system and pay full fees, which only 6% of parents do). They will therefore vote for higher expenditure when topping up is not allowed than when it is. So topping-up is not a good idea when the aim is to secure minimum standards for all. It is bound to lead to lower minimum standards and a more divided society.

A second problem with vouchers is that the state ends up paying for many people who now pay for themselves. This will happen under the present government's nursery scheme, and the same would occur under any voucher scheme for the period of compulsory education.

A third problem is that the control of quality becomes more difficult. The long-standing problems with the Youth Training Scheme are notorious, and these occurred even with sub-contracting. The problems with vouchers will be even greater.

We certainly want competition between different providers. In health this comes through the system of contracting with different hospitals. In education it already comes from competition among institutions for pupils and students. But this does not require a voucher system; it requires that the providers of finance (local education authorities, DfEE and funding councils) only pay their money for pupils and students who are there. Quality control is much easier through contract finance than through vouchers.

CONCLUSION

State spending has a vital role to play in any civilised society. Spending on health and education will have to grow faster than national income if people's preferences are to be respected. But other items, like pensions, can be reasonably contained as long as people are forced to provide for a supplementary private pension.

Public service should once more be an end for which people are proud to work. If properly used, this motive can deliver many of the 'sensitive' services, like health and education, more effectively than crude use of the profit motive. The public sector should not have to fight a constant rearguard action, which merely reduces morale and the quality of service.

Summary
- *Public expenditure exists partly to redistribute income and partly because some services (like health and education) cannot be paid for effectively through market mechanisms. The demand for many of these services rises faster than national income, putting upward pressure on the share of national income going into public expenditure.*

- *The present government is aiming at spending 40% of GDP or below compared with 41% today. There is no case for going below 40%, and a slightly higher figure may be necessary to achieve Labour's social objectives.*

- *Taxes are currently around 38% of GDP, and expenditure cannot exceed taxes by more than 2% of GDP without causing an undesirable increase in the ratio of public debt to GDP. It is too early to be sure of the future financial position. Labour's proposed Windfall Tax on utilities will provide some room for manoeuvre. But there may also need to be some over-indexation of taxes on anti-social activities (pollution, alcohol and smoking) in order to pay for social programmes and for tax cuts on low earners.*

- *In the longer term, public expenditure can be held near to 40% of GDP if the basic pension continues to be indexed to prices. But this minimal level of indexation is only tolerable if the guaranteed minimum income for pensioners rises in line with earnings. At the same time, people should be increasingly required to save for old age, thus building up a second income on top of the basic pension. They should also contribute to an insurance scheme to pay for long-term care in old age.*

- *Attempts to reduce public expenditure and improve efficiency through the Private Finance Initiative should be focused on capital projects rather than the provision of social services.*

- *Contracting-out of the provision of public services has in general gone far enough.*

- *Vouchers for individual consumers have many problems. They are not, in general, the way forward.*

6

Long-term Growth – Not Short-term Profit

We have a mission. We are prepared to go through difficult times and not just say, if in the next two years things are bad, we get out.
Jürgen Schrempp (Chairman, Daimler-Benz)

IF OUR ECONOMIC growth is too low, it is not only because we invest too little in people. We also invest too little in physical capital – machinery, buildings and infrastructure. In fact many of our companies will not invest at all unless the investment pays for itself within two or three years. This short-termism is deeply damaging and is a major cause of inadequate investment and insufficient growth.[1]

It stems from the incentives facing British managers. In Britain most major companies lack committed owners: they have no shareholder who owns a substantial block of shares and feels a committed partner in the enterprise. In Germany and Japan things are different. But in Britain, if things look bad, most owners start selling their shares, rather than doing something to get the company to perform better. Since the owners have little information about their companies, they are heavily influenced by the current level of profits – and so is the share price. If a manager does not want his firm to be taken over, he had better focus on maintaining its short-term profit – even if this means spending less on long-term development.

At the same time, because in Britain there are many willing sellers, an enterprising manager naturally becomes a deal-maker. He sees that the simplest way to expand his empire is to buy another company. From the point of view of the manager and his salary, this may be great. But from the point of view of the economy, the evidence is that much of this deal-making adds little value to the company as a whole and distracts managers from their main task, which should be to make the most of the productive potential of their existing enterprises.

We want managers to grow their companies through 'organic growth' and not mainly through acquisition. This 'organic growth' philosophy would be good even from the narrow point of view of the owners of capital. But it would also transform the outlook for thousands of workers, now threatened with downsizing as a result of a takeover. If managers focused more on organic growth, that would benefit all the stakeholders in the firm. The reverse is also true – if managers focused on the interests of workers as well as owners, the organic growth which resulted would be good for the economy as a whole.

I shall propose policy changes which would encourage more organic growth. But first we need a fuller explanation of the problem.

THE PROBLEM

Britain is a low investment country. If a country is poorer than other countries because it has low capital per head, then the appropriate response is for it to invest more of its income than richer countries. The higher investment rate will then produce a higher growth rate, leading to a process of catch-up. This is precisely what happened in countries like Japan: they

Long-term Growth – Not Short-term Profit

invested a higher share of income and in the process they adopted the technology of countries richer than them. And so they caught up.

By contrast Britain is not catching up, and one major reason for this is that we are not making the extra investment. On the contrary we have the lowest investment rate of any of the major countries shown in Table 14.[2] And even in the current recovery, investment has barely picked up – it is growing much more slowly than in previous recoveries.[3] Hence British workers continue to work with less capital than workers in other leading countries, while Japan makes faster strides through the increasing capital-intensity of its economy (see Figure 17).

Table 14: Investment as percentage of GDP, 1980–93

Japan	29.7
Italy	20.6
W. Germany	20.5
France	20.5
US	18.2
UK	17.3

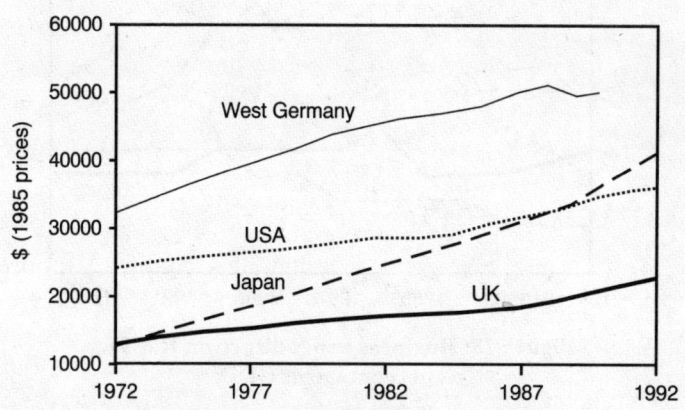

Figure 17: Capital stock per worker

Likewise our companies spend less on research and development (see Figure 18), which is another key route to rapid economic growth. It is a fallacy to suppose one can grow entirely by imitation, without major R & D of one's own. Companies which undertake their own R & D get a high average rate of return, though obviously some projects flop while others yield bonanzas.[4] In addition the rest of the economy gains by spillovers: the spillovers from business R & D (and even from more basic university research) accrue disproportionately to people in the same country. So our country as a whole suffers because of our lower level of business research and development.

Our low level of investment is not surprising when one considers the investment criteria used by many British companies. Two out of five British companies insist that an investment pay for itself within a small number of years, usually two or three years, ruling out many projects with good long-term returns.[5] How can one explain this degree of short-termism?

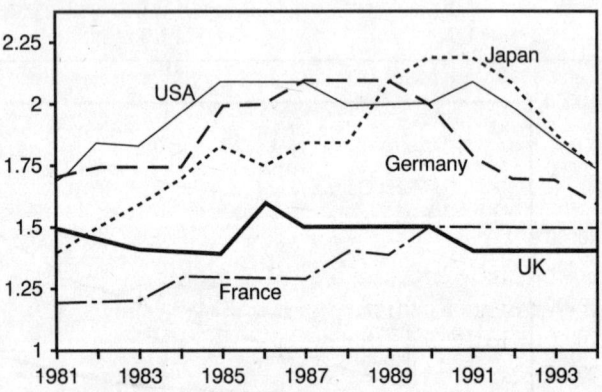

Figure 18: Business expenditure on R & D as percentage of GDP

BRITISH CAPITALISM

It stems from the nature of British capitalism. Most major British companies are quoted on the stock exchange, and of those that are quoted very few have a large shareholder. For example, among the largest quoted companies only 16% of British ones had any shareholder who owned more than a quarter of the shares. The comparable figure in France was 79%, and in Germany 85%[6] (and in Germany many major companies are not publicly quoted). If you have a large shareholding, you cannot easily dump your shares, and will probably take more interest in how the company is doing. If you have a small shareholding, you can easily sell a part of it and will feel much less committed to the firm.[7]

So in the German system the manager will generally have an owner who understands his business. In Britain this is less likely, and low short-term profits are likely to have a more devastating effect on the share price. This leaves the manager exposed to the threat of a hostile takeover.[8]

There is another reason why hostile takeovers are more common in Britain than elsewhere: the rights of owners are less restrained. In Germany directors are elected for fixed terms and cannot be removed. In the US too some 'shark-repellent' tactics are allowed, but they are not in Britain. Thus, whereas hostile takeovers are unknown in Germany and Japan, they are regular events in Britain, and to a lesser extent the US.

The result is a very different set of incentives for managers to perform. Everywhere the main pressure comes from competition, but in Britain the main additional pressure comes from the threat of takeover;[9] in the German–Japanese system it comes from the more reliable pressure of the committed owner.[10] The main characteristics of the two systems are shown in Table 15.

Of course the distinctions drawn in Table 15 are sharper

than those that apply in real life between British and German companies. For example twenty-five leading British companies have produced a report on 'Tomorrow's Company',[11] advocating a stakeholder approach to company management. And even our existing Companies Act says that 'the matters to which the directors are to have regard include the interests of the company's employees in general, as well as the interests of its members'. This goes well beyond the objective of maximising shareholder value, but since this is not always how the law has been interpreted a re-affirmation of this law would be helpful.

While some British companies have been relaxing the principle of shareholder value, some German companies have been moving closer to it. The clearest case is the troubled

Table 15: Types of firm

	Uncommitted owners	*Committed owners*
Whose interests count?	Shareholders	Shareholders, workers, etc.
Pressure on managers	Takeover threat	Existing owners, tradition of trusteeship
Criteria of success	Earnings per share	Productivity, employment, market power
Time-horizon	Short-term	Long-term
Method of adjustment	Buying and selling companies (incl. downsizing)	Organic growth (or decline)
Speed of response	Rapid	Slow
Industries favoured	Small-scale, high tech	Large scale, evolutionary

giant Daimler-Benz, whose chairman, Jürgen Schrempp, explained this shift in a recent interview with the *Financial Times*.[12] But he went on to contrast his company's philosophy sharply with that of General Electric in the US, which has made much money by buying and selling companies. 'We are coming from a totally different culture. We are not the cool portfolio managers. We have a mission. I want our people to identify with the company. We want to give them a stable perspective. We are prepared to go through difficult times and not just say, if in the next two years things are bad, we get out.' That just about says it all. Between the German–Japanese system and the Anglo-American there is a yawning gap.

It is impossible to say *a priori* which system is the more effective. Certainly the 'flexible' Anglo-American system makes it easier to raise venture capital and seems to favour the development of risky high-tech industries. But the German–Japanese system seems to be more effective for the solid development of major established industries. Overall, the judgment must be based on aggregate economic performance, and here Germany and Japan seem to have the edge. Their growth performance is better, and more of their populations benefit. It seems plausible that one reason for this is the stakeholder aspect of their systems of corporate governance.

THE DEAL-MAKING CULTURE

Perhaps the most worrying feature of the British system is the 'deal-making culture'.[13] The manager who buys another company almost invariably increases his own salary and improves his job security through diversification.[14] But on average his own shareholders do not gain any extra financial return.[15] There is often some immediate cost-cutting and downsizing as a result of a takeover, but there is no evidence that in the long-term productivity is on average improved by takeover.[16]

And indeed the same is true of downsizing in general. Thus Stephen Roach, the inventor of the phrase, has now admitted that, 'This approach is not a permanent solution. Tactics of open-ended downsizing and real wage compression are ultimately recipes for industrial extinction.' An easy thing to say after millions have been traumatised by the application of excessive cost-cutting.

There are certainly times when the only way to survive is to cut costs. But in good times it is generally better to consider what use can be made of the physical and human assets to hand, than to constantly jettison what you have. It is in this spirit that we have to approach the question of reform.

REFORM

This is a tricky area, where ill thought-out reform can easily produce undesirable side-effects. It is out of the question to simply import another country's institutions. Instead we need a shift of attitude among many managers, assisted by a few strategic changes in the legal framework.

There are three basic objectives:

- to liberate more managers to think and act long-term, by reducing the ease of takeover

- to provide different and more reliable pressures on managers to perform

- to ensure wider consideration of stakeholder interests in decision-making

These require changes in the rules related to:

- takeovers

- the disclosure of information

- corporate governance (i.e., the system for appointing and monitoring managers)

- worker participation

TAKEOVERS

Takeovers should become more costly. One possibility is a simple tax on all takeovers, but that is probably too drastic since the takeover threat must, under our present system, be the main sanction against inefficient top managers. A less drastic change, which is surely justified, is to increase the cost of layoffs for the period of a year after a takeover. All workers should have redundancy rights, irrespective of length of service, and all existing labour contracts should be taken over by the new owner. The reasoning is simple. If the takeover is truly efficient, it should be possible to compensate the main losers (those made redundant), without impeding the takeover. Only inefficient takeovers would be discouraged.

This proposal is current practice in the state of Pennsylvania. One result would be that managers and directors who had been appointed for a fixed term would continue to have the same security as before – a 'shark-repellent' device allowed in the US but not currently protected by British law. If a wholesale clear-out of directors is more difficult, a takeover is less attractive.

Another factor discouraging takeover would be the existence of some shares which have no voting rights. This device makes it easier for the original owner to raise money without risking loss of control of the enterprise. But in Britain the practice is discouraged by the stock exchange, in an obsessive effort to protect the rights of small shareholders. It should be accepted here as on the Continent. It should also be considered acceptable to issue blocks of voting shares to insiders.[17]

DISCLOSURE OF INFORMATION

Takeovers happen partly because they are easy, but also because existing owners often fail to appreciate the value of the company they own. As a result the share price becomes unreasonably low. The remedy is better information. Companies should have to publicly provide a much fuller range of information than at present. This could include data on relations with customers, suppliers, and employees, as well as on R & D. Some of this is already recommended in the code of practice proposed by the Cadbury Committee,[18] but it should be further institutionalised. While it is always a hassle to provide information, it is in the long run the only way of being sure you are understood.[19]

A different, and more difficult, issue is whether a large shareholder should be allowed to get more information than other shareholders – so that he can apply more effective pressure on the management to perform. At present this is discouraged by the rules against insider trading, but the gain in efficiency from a relaxation here might well offset the disadvantage experienced by the small shareholders.

Another line of thought is the efficiency audit. The largest US pension fund, Calpers, is calling for institutions which invest in British companies to set up a joint audit body which would investigate companies whose long-term performance looked bad. There should be a Council of Institutional Investors which would publish reports and exert whatever other pressure they could on under-performing companies. To prevent free riding, membership would be mandatory for all funds investing in the UK.

CORPORATE GOVERNANCE

This brings us to the question of formal changes in the rules of corporate governance. How can effective pressure be brought on top managers to perform well? It is not efficient if the only sanction is the fear of takeover. There must be more on-going monitoring and accountability.

The German system relies upon two-tier boards – a supervisory board (rather like trustees) and an executive board (consisting of managers). Our system has a unified board, but including some non-executive directors (NEDs) who are not managers. This is not required by law but it has become the custom. The Cadbury Committee recommends that there should always be at least three NEDs, and that they should be nominated by a committee on which executives were in a minority.

The problem is that NEDs can so easily be in the pocket of the executives. This might be avoided if the Council of Institutional Investors developed a list of suitable people and encouraged under-performing firms to appoint NEDs from this list. The Council could also help to train NEDs, so that for some people this might become a full-time activity, as with auditors.

WORKER PARTICIPATION

And what about the workers? It is quite clear that employees have a stronger interest in the health of a company than most of the owners do.[20] But they often lack the necessary information and an appropriate forum for expressing their views. Two key proposals could provide workers with a better 'voice'.

The European Union's Social Chapter provides for works councils, for any company of size operating in more than one European country.[21] The balance of evidence is that works councils are good for productivity.[22] They are a good way for workers to bring their own insights to bear, without infringing the ultimate prerogative of managers to manage. For this reason (and others) we should adopt the European Social Chapter.

Employees should also be encouraged to become owners, through Employee Share Ownership Plans (ESOPs). These already encourage employee commitment. But they could also be used to focus employee know-how to improve the management of the company, if employee owners were to form an association that functioned as an active shareholder. This should be encouraged.

The proposals set out above are not individually dramatic, but they would go far to encourage the development of committed ownership in Britain, as well as enhancing the influence of workers on decision-making.[23]

COMPETITION POLICY

There is one further spur to efficient management which we have not mentioned yet, though it is surely the most important. This is the spur of competition.[24]

Not everyone believes this. There is an alternative view that market power is good for efficiency because it guarantees a return on innovation and investment. And, it is also pointed out, fewer firms will tend to be bigger, giving economies of scale. This 'Schumpeterian' view, which used to be popular in the 1960s and 1970s, gave rise to the idea that countries would do well to create 'national champions' in key industries.

But the history of 'national champions' (British Leyland, for example) has been chequered, and at the same time a weight of evidence has accumulated that shows that competition is good for productivity and for growth. For example, in Japan the industries which have been most successful on the international stage are those where there is fierce domestic rivalry between a number of companies (see Table 16). The finding in favour of competition emerges from many systematic statistical comparisons among companies, among industries, and among countries.[25]

British policy has not been tough enough on competition – nor predictable enough. This is true of policy towards monopoly and of policy towards price-rigging cartels. As regards monopoly, the test of a merger or takeover should always be 'Does it significantly reduce competition?' One reason why so few mergers or takeovers are currently stopped is that, for a merger to be stopped, three separate parties must agree:

- The Office of Fair Trading (OFT) must refer the case to the Monopolies and Mergers Commission (MMC)

- The MMC must rule against it

- The Secretary of State for Trade and Industry must accept the MMC ruling

This is one party too many. The Secretary of State should lay down the criteria for decisions, but have nothing to do with individual cases. Instead the OFT should be turned into a clear prosecuting body and the MMC into a tribunal.[26]

But mergers and acquisitions are not the only problem: two companies do not have to merge in order to act uncompetitively. They can fix prices, or agree on other forms of restrictive practice. Amazingly, such behaviour is not automatically illegal under British law – specific cases have to be brought to court by the OFT and may then be banned by court order. A 1989 White Paper recommended that these practices should be automatically illegal in Britain, as they are in European inter-state trade according to Articles 85 and 86

Table 16: Number of major rivals in various Japanese industries

Automobiles	9
Cameras	15
Copiers	14
Motorcycles	4
Steel	5
TV sets	15

of the Treaty of Rome. This White Paper proposal should be quickly put into the law, with a system of heavy penalties. To make the system effective the OFT should have much greater power to descend on companies suspected of anti-competitive activities.

SMALL FIRMS

So far we have focused mainly on how to increase long-term thinking and competitive behaviour among our larger companies. But larger companies with over 500 employees produce less than half the output of the business sector. The rest is produced in small and medium enterprises (SMEs) – see Table 17. They are enormously important to our economy.

Table 17: Small business employs nearly half the workforce

No. of employees in enterprise	Percentage of workers in this size of enterprise
Under 10	26
10–99	21
100–499	18
500+	35
Total	100

How can we help these firms to perform well? They are subject to a frightening rate of business failure – some 10% a year.[27] In most cases this reflects financial difficulties and often weakness of business planning. Is there anything that should be done to help on these fronts?

There are already many government initiatives in this area, which the government is trying to co-ordinate through its new structure of Business Links. But major problems will continue. It will always be difficult for banks to know whether a small business has real prospects. Five steps would help enormously:

- We need to be moving towards a position where (as in Germany) anyone running a small business has some basic business qualification. We need to develop this qualification and its delivery. If a person holds this basic Financial Management Certificate, it would provide an important signal to a potential lender.

- We need a much more powerful network of local business organisation, which can provide technical support for small businesses but also set quality standards. In Germany this is provided by the local Chamber of Commerce, for which membership is compulsory. The Chamber sets quality standards, organises business advice and co-ordinates training. If we adopted this solution, the Training and Enterprise Councils (TECs) would be subsumed into the new local Chambers of Commerce. They would thus become more truly representative of local business interests, rather than being quangos appointed in Westminster. And clearly the knowledge of local business developed through the Chamber would greatly assist banks, as they tried to support the growth points in the local economy.[28]

- Regional development agencies can also help to promote industrial development on a regional basis, by seedcorn finance of interlinked developments – and by lobbying for the necessary infrastructure.

- Equally important at a more technical level, the national industry associations need to organise networks which promote good practice in underperforming firms. The Society of Motor Manufacturers has paved the way here with its industry forum that defines good practice and supplies technical assistance, for a fee.

- A final, more tentative, idea comes from Italy, where groups of like-minded small businesses guarantee each other's debts on certain conditions. If a member of the consortium wants to borrow money, the consortium scrutinises the proposal and decides whether to endorse it or not. If it has been endorsed, the business then finds it much easier to borrow money, and to do so on reasonable terms.

CONCLUSION

The future of our economy ultimately lies with business. The state cannot produce growth, but it can provide the right incentives and structures. Our economy will do much better if we give incentives for the organic growth of enterprises, and this will benefit capitalists and workers alike. We need to be more vigilant against actions which restrict competition. And we need to provide the right supportive framework for medium and small business, which produces over half of business output.

Long-term Growth – Not Short-term Profit

Summary

- In Britain most large companies have no major committed shareholders. Most shareholders are willing to sell their shares at short notice, and at the same time a new buyer has unlimited rights to reorganise the company and 'downsize' its workforce. So hostile takeover is common.

- Hostile takeover does not, on average, improve long-run performance. But the threat of it forces managers to pay undue attention to short-term profit, often at the expense of long-term development.

- The ease of takeover encourages managers to develop their empires by acquisition rather than by organic growth.

- The aims of reform should be to discourage inefficient takeovers, improve other methods of motivating managers, and encourage organic growth for the benefit of all stakeholders. Reforms are needed in relation to takeovers, disclosure of information, non-executive directors, worker participation, and product market competition.

- **Takeovers**. After a takeover all employment contracts should remain in force, and all workers laid off should be entitled to compensation even if only recently hired. If those who lose from takeovers are compensated, this will not prevent efficient takeovers going through. Companies should also be allowed to issue non-voting shares to outsiders, in order to concentrate control of the company.

- **Disclosure**. Firms should be required to provide more extensive information on their performance and plans. The investing institutions should set up a Council of Institutional Investors to undertake efficiency audits of companies that seem to have poor long-term performance.

- **Non-executive directors.** *There should be at least three, selected by a nominating committee independent of the executives. The Council of Institutional Investors should assist in the development and training of potential non-executive directors.*

- **Worker participation.** *All large companies should have 'European' Works Councils. Employee share ownership should be encouraged, and employee owners should organise to be represented as shareholders.*

- **Competition policy.** *To promote business efficiency, there should be stricter policies to promote competition (and no attempt to develop 'national champions'). Price-fixing and related restrictive practices should be simply illegal, as they are banned in inter-state trade by the Treaty of Rome.*

- *Medium and small businesses produce over half of business output. To raise standards and help these firms raise money, three steps would help greatly. There should be a basic Certificate of Financial Management which ultimately would become a sine qua non for running a small business (unless the person already had a better qualification). In addition all businesses in an area should belong to the local Chamber of Commerce which would incorporate existing TECs; these Chambers would provide the structure for maintaining standards, disseminating information and co-ordinating training. And at the more technical level, national industry associations should define standards and provide technical assistance, for a fee.*

7

No More Boom and Bust

Our stability is but balance, and conduct lies
In masterful administration of the unforeseen.
         Robert Bridges, 'Testament of Beauty'

MOST PEOPLE WANT security, or if they seek adventure they want to do so on their own terms. They do not want to be laid off or forced to change job because their firm is in trouble. Though some job insecurity is inevitable, as one firm is replaced by another and industries become obsolete, the government can have a major effect on the insecurity caused by aggregate fluctuations of the economy – as boom gives way to bust.

Businesses also place a huge value on stability. They want a stable market, not one that is see-sawing unpredictably. And they want low and stable interest rates.

Britain in the last eighteen years has not been good at generating either stable markets or stable interest rates. Figure 19 shows the annual changes in output. These were anything but steady and, if we look at the variation in these growth rates, it is larger than in any other major country.[1] This is not surprising since we have had two deep recessions, in 1980–81 and in 1991–92. These recessions were both largely the result of government policy, and illustrate its power to do good or ill.

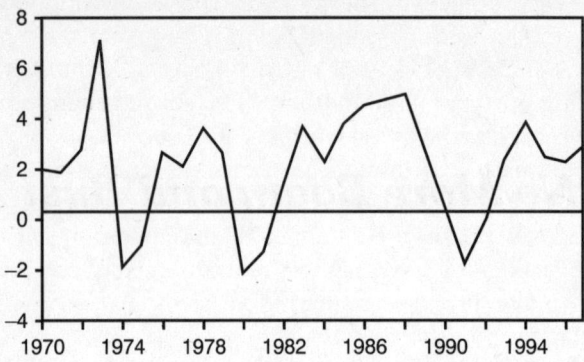

Figure 19: Unstable output

The issue now facing this country is how to do better. One part of this question is: would we do better to leave our monetary policy to the European Bank by joining the single currency? But before we embark on that issue we should first clarify how our present system of running our economy works – or does not work – and what other ways of improvement are open to us.

The government's two main instruments for controlling the economy are monetary policy and the budget. Monetary policy means in essence the fixing of short-term interest rates, which is done by the Chancellor who consults monthly with the Governor of the Bank of England. Both monetary policy and the budget have profound effects on fluctuations in the level of unemployment. But they cannot affect the long-run level of unemployment, averaged for example over a decade, because that is determined by structural features of the labour market. If the government attempts to increase the number of jobs beyond this sustainable number through running a higher budget deficit or lower interest rates, then employers will experience labour shortages and start to bid up wages. At the same time workers will feel stronger and press for higher wage increases. The result will be ever-increasing inflation, such as we have experienced in the past. So the main function of monetary policy and the budget balance is to reduce the *fluctuations* in the level of output, rather than to affect its average level taking one year with another.[2] The second main objective is to secure a low average level of inflation.

At one time it was thought possible to secure some extra output at the cost of some higher inflation. But this option disappeared at the end of the 1960s as the public became wise to what was happening. Now almost all economists believe that you can only secure a permanent increase in jobs beyond the sustainable level at the cost not of extra inflation but of *ever-increasing* inflation. So the discussion of whether we are willing to tolerate extra inflation as the price of extra jobs has become obsolete. Monetary and fiscal policy have to operate against the background of the unemployment constraint; it is only other kinds of measures that can shift that constraint – and we shall come back to that at the end of the chapter. The main role of monetary and fiscal policy is to minimise fluctuations in output around the sustainable level. Let us examine the record, in order to see how it can be improved.

THE RECORD OF INSTABILITY

When Mrs Thatcher came to power, inflation was running at 14% – roughly the European average. The following year it shot up to 20% (see Figure 20), largely due to an ill-judged increase in VAT (which cuts in Income Tax were meant to offset). To attack this high inflation, interest rates were increased to 15% – see Figure 21. These high rates, plus the UK's new-found oil wealth, pushed up the pound (which was floating) to the dizzy height of $2.40. Output fell sharply and unemployment soared.

The government's next move was to loosen monetary policy but tighten fiscal policy. In due course output began to recover from the level it had reached. And this high rate of growth went on for a very long time. Eventually it got out of hand. The government believed there had been a 'Thatcher miracle' and persuaded the public likewise. So families spent and spent, on borrowed money. Deregulation in the early 1980s had encouraged a spending spree – most limits on bank lending and bank reserves had been abolished, and building societies too were allowed to borrow in the capital market. Once people became convinced that high growth would go on

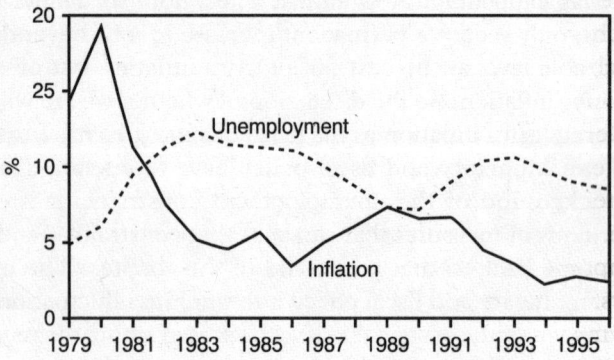

Figure 20: Unemployment and inflation

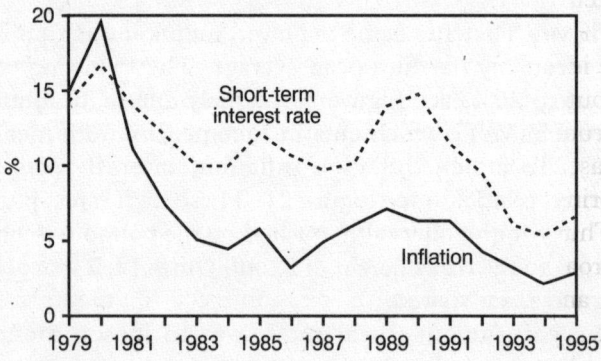

Figure 21: Short-term interest rates and inflation

for ever they went out and borrowed in order to spend. At the same time interest rates were held down to stop the pound appreciating.

Then suddenly the government noticed that inflation was creeping up, as mainstream economists had always predicted it eventually would – see Figure 21. The whole policy went into reverse, and interest rates were raised. Once people realised they had overborrowed, they cut their spending sharply and we went into a second major recession. At the same time the pound joined the European Exchange Rate Mechanism at the overvalued rate of DM 2.95 to the pound – which was no good for our ability to compete in foreign markets.

Recovery from the last recession began in 1993, aided by the exchange rate collapse on Black Wednesday of 16 September 1992 which greatly improved our ability to compete. By late 1996 unemployment was down to 8% – which compares with its average level of 8.6% over the last eight years.[3] It is extremely difficult to tell how much further unemployment can continue to fall without inflation beginning to rise.

The guiding star of current government policy is the inflation target. Monetary and fiscal policy together are given the objective of ensuring that inflation is within the target band of 1–4% two years down the road, with a preference for 2½%. The idea is that inflation depends on the level of output, and output depends on monetary and fiscal policy. So these two instruments together must be used to prevent output growing so fast that inflation takes off, and output has then to be cut to bring inflation into line.

Thus the objective is a 'soft landing'. We should if possible approach the critical level of unemployment in a circumspect way and then stay there – avoiding the fluctuations of the past.

MONETARY POLICY

In general this is the right approach.[4] But there are well-known temptations, which have affected governments in the past and will surely affect them in the future. The temptation is this: if a government stokes up a boom, the benefits in extra output and more jobs come first, while the costs in extra inflation come later. Any government will be tempted to reflate before an election to get the extra jobs and the extra popularity – hoping that by the time of the next election but one, people will have forgotten the inflation that happened in the meantime. This builds an inflationary bias into the system.[5]

One way to deal with this is to hand over monetary policy to a non-political body like the Bank of England, who would be less subject to these temptations. This has been the system in the USA and Germany since the war. The Federal Reserve Board and the Bundesbank set national short-term interest rates without political interference. There is certainly some evidence that independent central banks tend to produce lower inflation.[6] Many countries have moved to full independence, including New Zealand and France; most other European countries are moving rapidly in that direction.

We ourselves have taken tentative steps in the same direction. The Chancellor of the Exchequer now has a formal monthly meeting with the Governor of the Bank of England, whose minutes are published six weeks later. Monetary policy announcements usually follow these meetings, and the discussions there are conducted against the background of the Bank's Inflation Report which includes its forecasts of inflation in the next two years.

Some people thought that with this degree of openness it would be impossible for the Chancellor to reject the Governor's advice. He has in fact done so on a number of occasions, because he judged that the inflation risks were lower than the Bank thought. The sluggishness of the economy in 1996 has seemed to justify the Chancellor's willingness to cut interest rates, but 1997 promises to bring faster growth and at some point interest rates will have to rise.[7]

So should we move to full independence for the Central Bank? If we adopt the European single currency, we shall have to do so. The European Central Bank would then make our monetary policy, and the Bank of England would be one of its branches, with our Governor on its governing body. As I shall explain in the next chapter, I think this is the way Britain should go. But even the present monetary system does a lot more to help keep the government honest than the system we had in the past. It would be further improved if the internal procedures of the Bank were more formal, so as to reduce the highly personal image of policy-making.

THE BUDGET

So much for monetary policy. What of the budget? The main limit on the budget deficit, or public sector borrowing requirement (PSBR), is the need to avoid an inordinate rise in the public debt. This would push up interest rates and undermine confidence. However, there is obviously no problem if the public debt increases in line with the national income – since higher national income will yield higher taxes from which to finance the debt. Thus a sensible objective is to stabilise the ratio of debt to GDP.[8] So how much extra debt could be issued? The existing net debt of the government is about 40% of annual GDP.[9] If national income grows in nominal terms by 5% a year, the debt could safely grow at a rate of 5% – in other words it could grow by 2% of GDP (5% of 40%). Thus the deficit could average 2% of GDP. That would be a quite safe limit, which, if followed on average over the cycle, would prevent debt growing relative to GDP.

Unfortunately, achieving that limit, averaged over the business cycle, is not going to be easy. For in the year up to April 1997, the forecast for the deficit is 4% of GDP.[10] The trend is downward, as Figure 22 shows. But it may not be easy to

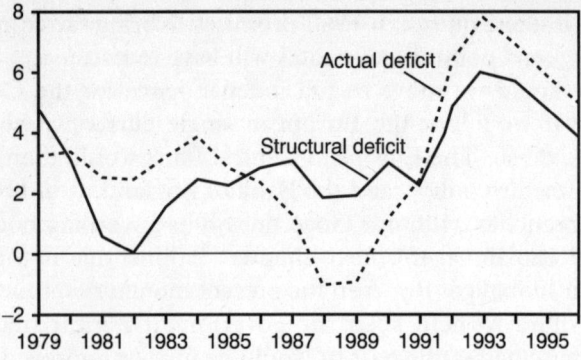

Figure 22: Budget deficit as percentage of GDP

achieve Labour's social objectives without some further tax revenue. The proposed Windfall Tax on utilities will provide some leeway, but more may be needed (see Chapter 5).

The reason for this dilemma is easy to see from the line in Figure 22 marked 'Structural deficit'. This line calculates the deficit, adjusted for whether the economy is in boom or slump so that tax receipts differ from their average level at existing tax rates. A structural deficit of around 2% of GDP is fine. But the 1991 tax-cutting Budget led to an enormous deficit expansion in 1992. This was shameless electioneering. As a result the Tories have been forced into a series of tax increases to undo their previous mistakes. The outlook still looks difficult, though it is now too early to know whether extra revenue will be needed.

One key variable could improve the whole situation. If unemployment could after all go on falling without inflation increasing, then we could get our further tax revenue financed by growth rather than by having to increase tax rates.

INCREASING SUSTAINABLE EMPLOYMENT

How could this happen? We have already discussed two of the main policies needed to cut unemployment – eliminating low-skill, and shifting from passive benefits to active help for those out of work. But the first will take some time to affect unemployment, and the second must be phased in. A third approach would complement these and could have a speedier effect.

Unemployment is lower, other things being equal, in those countries where there is some national consensus about the rate of growth of pay. For where such a consensus exists it is possible for unemployment to be low without inflation immediately increasing.

The most striking example of this approach is in the German bloc of countries (Germany, Austria and the Netherlands). Germany has a regular annual cycle which begins when the Council of Economic Advisers forecasts the inflationary implications of different possible wage settlements. This happens in November, and there are also forecasts from the five economic institutes which lead to a serious national debate about what level of average wage settlement makes sense. The employers then agree a common line, and, when negotiations begin soon after, this has a major effect on the first settlement – which is generally then followed throughout the economy. Japanese pay settlements happen in a similar way, and inflation remains low despite low unemployment.

We need a system more like these. There should be a formal National Economic Assessment which comes up with suggestions for an acceptable average rate of wage settlement (after allowing for likely earnings drift). There should then be a serious attempt among employers to hold to this line. Clearly some firms have special circumstances – the need to attract new staff or to buy out poor working practices – but this apart, there is no reason why a firm should pay more than the average rate of increase. If all firms try to be better employers than their neighbours, the only outcome is leap-frogging wages, which then leads to leap-frogging pricing. When this happens, the Bank of England has no alternative but to pull on the brakes.

The problem is a serious one, because each employer's pay settlement has a 'demonstration' effect on other workers (even when it is based on good productivity performance in the particular firm). So Labour should galvanise the CBI (and Institute of Directors) into suitable forms of employer solidarity. One possibility would be a CBI Committee that issued proposals and expected explanations from those who disregarded them.[11]

If we move aggressively towards measures such as these, we can help to kill two birds with one stone: we can have lower unemployment, and we can collect more taxes to pay for social goods without having to raise tax rates. There can be no question of compulsion, but there is a real role for consensus in a well-functioning society.

CONCLUSION

Among the world's major nations, Britain has the worst postwar record of boom and bust. This is mainly due to bad monetary policy, which should therefore be further divorced from the political process. We also have an unemployment rate that is intolerably high (when averaged over boom and bust). This cannot be reduced by simply boosting demand. But it can be reduced by developing skills, through active labour market policy, and by greater national consensus over pay.

Summary

- *Unstable economic management (especially monetary policy) has given Britain two of the deepest five recessions in G7 countries since 1950.*

- *Monetary policy is less subject to electoral pressures when central banks have more independence.*

- *The budget deficit should not exceed 2% of GDP on average over the cycle.*

- *If average unemployment over the cycle could be reduced, this would raise more taxes and ease the pressures on the budget.*

- *To permit a lower level of unemployment without inflation increasing, we ought to have a National Economic Assessment of what average level of wage settlements is in the national interest. The CBI should develop methods for pressing its members to stay in line, unless they are in exceptional circumstances.*

8

Joining Europe's Currency

> *It is said that the emu cannot fly, but neither can it go backwards.*
>
> Karl Otto Pöhl

BY EARLY 1998 BRITAIN will have to make a major decision which will affect our future economic stability and our whole position in the world. We shall have to decide whether to join the single European currency.[1]

For most people the key issue is jobs. Is there a risk to jobs, which the advantages of joining cannot outweigh? Let us first look at how the single currency would work, and then at the pros and cons.

THE PROPOSAL

The current plan is for a single European currency to come into existence in January 1999. It may of course get delayed, but at present it is odds on that it will go ahead and include at least France, Germany, Benelux and Austria. By Autumn 1997 we have to decide whether we want to renew our opt-out or whether we wish to be considered with all the other candidates for membership.

What would membership mean? We should lose our

separate currency, and our interest rates would be set by the new European Central Bank based in Frankfurt. The Governor of the Bank of England would be one of the governors of the European Central Bank, and his vote, with the others, would determine the course of European interest rates.[2]

The new European currency would be the Euro. The separate national currencies would not disappear from sight till 2002, but from January 1999 their exchange rates would be locked irrevocably both to each other and to the Euro. Initially only government debt will be denominated in Euros, but over the following three years all other obligations and contracts will be changed over to Euros. Then at the beginning of 2002, Euro notes and coins will come into circulation, and by the middle of that year all national notes and coins will have been exchanged for Euros.

Soon after the next general election we have to decide whether we want to join this system, and then, in April 1998, the leaders of Europe's governments (presided over by Britain) will decide which countries satisfy the criteria entitling them to join. Britain is likely to satisfy most of the main 'convergence criteria' laid down in the Maastricht Treaty. These are that by 1997 a country has:

(i) a budget deficit under 3% of GDP, or nearly so;
(ii) a public debt below 60% of annual GDP, or approaching that level sufficiently fast;
(iii) compared with the three lowest inflation countries, inflation not higher by more than 1.5%, and long-term interest rates not higher by more than 2%

There is one other criterion: that the currency has been within the 'normal operating margins of the ERM' for two years. This criterion is unclear[3] but it would probably not be invoked against a Labour government. The choice will be ours.

So what are the advantages and disadvantages of joining?

ADVANTAGES

On the economic side there are two sorts of arguments in favour. The first five relate to why Britain should favour the creation of a single currency; the rest relate to why we should join if it happens (even if we didn't want it to happen).

- Under a single currency, there would be no national currencies and therefore **no cost of changing or trading currencies**. (This saving is probably quite small – less than ½% of GDP.)

- There would almost certainly be **lower average inflation**, since the European Bank will be more independent than even an independent national central bank. The bank will be based in Frankfurt and will surely acquire a strong dose of the anti-inflationary culture that is commonplace in Germany.

- There would almost certainly be **lower interest rates** – partly due to lower inflation and partly due to the absence of exchange rate risk, which otherwise makes foreigners require a 'risk premium' when they lend to Britain. We already see how French and German long-term bond yields have converged while British yields in November 1996 were roughly 2 percentage points higher.

- There would be **fewer problems from uncertain and variable exchange rates** which cause such difficulties for exporting companies.[4] If exchange rates change, this changes the ratio between a firm's receipts from foreign trade and its domestic costs. Uncertainty about all this discourages trade, but more seriously the changes themselves may destroy whole tracts of the economy. Experience with floating exchange rates since the early 1970s has shown that these can easily be driven up and down by speculation, in a way that has no real economic rationale but can wipe out firms and even whole sectors of industry. Thousands of firms went under when sterling was overvalued in 1980 and again in 1991, and the same happened in the US when the dollar was overvalued in 1985. If we continue to float, this could happen again.

- **Our record of monetary stability is poor**. British policy-makers of both parties have managed to inflict on Britain three of the seven biggest recessions in G7 countries since the 1950s. With interest rates made elsewhere, we could hope to be spared the worst of these shocks.

These are reasons why we might have wished to propose a currency union. But the present situation goes beyond that. The single currency is likely to happen anyway, and there are serious dangers in being left out:

- There is the **danger of losing markets and investment** if we fail to join the club. People tend to trade with others who use the same currency. So non-Europeans wanting to invest in Europe will tend to plant their factories in countries belonging to the club. This non-European direct investment in Britain has been an important spur to modernisation and we should not put it at risk.

- There is also the danger of **losing political influence in Europe**. This could cost us economically, as the current BSE negotiations show.

- Then there is the **risk to the City**.[5] It is difficult to know how far the City might lose business if we were outside the common currency. It may not be a major risk, but why take it at all?

- And finally there are the **major dangers in leaving this**

matter unresolved. All uncertainty discourages investment – people wait to see what will happen. In many ways it would be better to decide one way or the other than to leave the matter for endless debate, discussion and negotiation.

Disadvantages

So there are major advantages to joining now, which are tabulated in Table 18. Against these there is one clear disadvantage. If Britain is hit by a shock that does not affect the rest of Europe in the same way, we have to fight the shock with one hand tied behind our back – we cannot set our own interest rates.

Suppose foreigners' appetite for British goods falls, and British unemployment starts rising. With a floating exchange rate we could re-invigorate demand by cutting interest rates –

Table 18: Balance sheet for the Euro

Advantages of entry
No cost of changing currencies
Lower average inflation
Lower interest rates
Less uncertainty about exchange rates
Fewer output fluctuations due to fluctuating real exchange rates
Fewer output fluctuations due to local monetary disturbances
Better market access
More influence in Europe
Fewer risks for the City
Ending uncertainty about our policy

Disadvantages of entry
Less ability to offset local shocks to real demand
Possible deflationary bias at the beginning

which would itself stimulate domestic demand, as well as lowering the value of the pound so that the demand for exports recovered. Under the single currency we would not be able to do that.

How serious a problem is the absence of this key policy lever? It is exactly the same as the problem facing, say, California. If the demand for computers falls, California is hit more than the rest of America. But the Federal Reserve will respond very little to a problem that is limited to California. So what happens in California?

If the shock is permanent, its economy goes through a period of unemployment. This reduces real wages, thus improving competitiveness, and in addition some workers decide to leave. By contrast, if California had its own currency and a flexible exchange rate, it could have devalued and thus restored competitiveness without so much intervening unemployment. This would have certainly been preferable. Similarly, if the shock is temporary, California goes through a period of unemployment which could have been shortened if it had control of its own interest rates.

The same argument also applies in reverse. If California experiences a rise in demand for its goods, it cannot revalue its currency so as to reduce the upwards pressure on domestic prices. Instead, it has to experience higher prices which eventually reduce its competitiveness and bring its economy back into balance.

Even so, no one advocates that California should have its own currency. This suggests that the real problems caused by regional shocks are not generally intolerable. However, some people say that the US analogy is not relevant to Europe, because in the US there are federal transfers to hard-hit states – a bad argument since hard-hit countries in Europe can run budget deficits to offset shocks. But it is true that Americans are more willing to move between regions than Europeans are between countries, and this eases the change in real wages that would otherwise be needed in response to a permanent shock.

On the other hand the US states are *more* prone to region-specific shocks than the states of Europe. This is because there is much more regional specialisation in the US than there is in Northern Europe – with many industries concentrated in a very few US states. By contrast the economies of Northern Europe are much more similar to each other (see Table 19) and therefore less vulnerable to localised shocks.[6]

Table 19: Distribution of car production across four main regions (%)

Within USA		Within Europe	
Midwest	67	Germany	38
South	25	France	31
West	5	Italy	18
North-East	3	UK	13
Total	100	Total	100

There has however been one huge regional shock, from which Europe is still recovering – the shock of German reunification. The rebuilding of the East enormously increased the demand for German output. One solution would have been to allow an appreciation of the D-Mark relative to the French franc, so that foreigners found German goods more expensive and bought less of them, thus reducing the overheating of the German economy. This would have solved the problem of inflationary pressure on prices inside Germany.

However, the French government would not accept the idea of a German appreciation (thus behaving as if the franc and the D-Mark were already one currency). In consequence German prices inevitably rose in response to excess demand. The Bundesbank was unwilling to accept this inflation, and therefore raised interest rates. This eventually imposed enough deflation on Germany to bring inflation under control. But it caused serious unemployment in France. This is a clear example of how the linking of currencies can cause problems when there is a shock to one country and not to others in the same currency area.

So isn't this recent experience of the ERM a sufficient argument against a single currency? After all, Britain clearly gained by leaving the ERM in 1992. Why lock in again?

JOINING EMU IS NOT RETURNING TO THE ERM

There are three basic points:

- Britain joined the ERM in 1990 at a **grossly overvalued exchange rate**, at which we could simply not compete. Now we have a more competitive exchange rate at which we could safely lock in.

- **The EMU is quite different from the ERM**. EMU will not allow a single country to set the pattern of interest rates for the rest of Europe. By contrast now, under the ERM, Germany in effect provides the anchor currency and all the other countries have to peg to the D-Mark. The others therefore have to follow German interest rates. Under the EMU, interest rates would be set by the European Central Bank in the interest of Europe as a whole. Even so, one country might be struck by a major shock which did not affect the others. So far there has been only the shock of German reunification, but one cannot rule out another such shock, and it might hit Britain. If it did, what would we do?

- We still have one independent string to our bow – **the budget**. We can use that to offset the shock. To a large extent we could in fact vary taxes to mimic the effect of changes in interest rates; we could for example vary the tax treatment of mortgage interest in order to offset a housing boom or slump.

It is important that this flexibility be permitted within the European rules relating to fiscal deficits (the so-called 'stability pact'). For most of the arguments for external interference in fiscal policy carry little weight. Two main arguments are offered.

First, if governments are imprudent, they may get into trouble and come to the authorities for bail-outs. But bail-outs are banned in the Treaty. This means that a government might default. A default, it is said, could cause a banking crisis if some banks had too much of the defaulting country's debt. But this problem should be dealt with by proper prudential supervision of banks, so that they do not become too exposed to risky debt. It does not require interference with a member government's budget.

The second argument is that, if a government borrows more, it will force up interest rates for everyone. This is true. But if any group of people borrow more – for example to improve their homes – they push up interest rates for everyone. That is not a case of market failure – it is precisely how market prices work, by reflecting the urgency of people's needs. In the US there are no federal rules which limit the deficits of the US states.[7] So why should there be in Europe?[8]

On these grounds we ought not to be too happy about the limits on budgets in the proposed fiscal 'stability pact'. But we are better placed to argue the case from inside than if we fail to join. And, even if limits are imposed, we can retain freedom of short-term manoeuvre if we keep our average deficit low enough.

What we could never escape, and would not want to escape, would be the regular consultations between the European Central Bank and the Council of Ministers about the balance between monetary and fiscal policy at the pan-European level. Whatever a country's choice about its budget deficit, and thus its long-run growth rate, all countries have an interest in short-term macroeconomic stability. This requires co-ordination between Treasuries and Central Banks. We should be present at those discussions.

Another argument, which can still be heard, we should strongly reject. This is that Britain is inevitably a high-inflation country, so that losing the ability to devalue will plunge us into permanent recession, unable to sell our goods. That is absurd. We have had low inflation for some years now and one major purpose of joining the single currency is to keep it that way.

NO CASE FOR WAITING

In my opinion the case for joining is overwhelming. But when? There is a vocal school who favour entry, but not yet. They offer a number of economic arguments:

- We cannot join till our **productivity** is more similar to Germany's, since we shall not be able to compete. This is quite wrong. Our competitiveness depends upon our productivity *relative* to our wages. Unless our wages are too high, we can compete quite well, even if our productivity is lower. Indeed we do so already, and our current exchange rate makes us highly competitive with Germany. This makes it a good moment to enter. The only danger is the longer term one that British unions will, under the Euro, seek parity of pay with Europe, even if our productivity is lower. But if productivity and pay really had to be uniform inside a currency union, different currencies would be needed in different parts of the UK and in different states of the USA. This argument clearly does not work.

- There should be **real convergence of unemployment rates**. But unemployment is determined in the long run by different forces from those which determine inflation and economic stability – mainly by the structure of the labour market, which always differs between countries. A non-inflationary reduction of unemployment in all the countries of Europe is essential, and there are labour market policies that can achieve it. But that is a totally independent issue from the regulation of the UK's financial affairs: the case for joining the single currency rests on what it will do to inflation, growth, economic fluctuations and the volume of trade.

- We should wait till our economy is **more like the Europeans'**. This again is wrong. As we become more integrated, our economy may well become more different from others' – just as the different states within the US vary more in economic structure than the separate nation states of Northern Europe. Differences in economic structure provide no argument for delay. It is true that some of our institutions (like our floating rate mortgages) increase our responsiveness to interest rates, but this point can easily be exaggerated. If we wait for major institutional change, we could wait a long time.

- **Why not wait while the others go through the teething problems**. This is a serious issue. There is clearly a danger that in its early years the European Central Bank will wish to be excessively deflationary, in order to establish its credibility. In fact the Bundesbank itself has been excessively deflationary in the last few years, and what Europe now needs is monetary expansion to go with the necessary fiscal contraction. Some people say that this is so unlikely that we should, for the time being, stay out.

I disagree, because Britain will be influenced by what happens to the European economy whether we are in or out.

Better therefore to be inside, influencing what happens. More importantly, the early years will set the ground rules which will operate for many years after. We need to ensure a proper role for the Council of Ministers. If the Central Bank is too deflationary, the Council should argue with them.

There are major issues about how the Bank will operate – what targets it will have, and how these will be influenced from outside. Under the Maastricht Treaty, exchange rate policy lies with the Council of Ministers – just as it lies with the central government in the US and each existing European country. So in this sense no central bank is fully independent. The way in which the relations between the European Central Bank and the Council of Ministers develops is crucial, and Britain should be in there influencing it. When we failed to join the Common Market in 1957, we lost influence over Europe's agricultural policy, for which we continue to suffer. Let us not make a similar mistake now.

One further point. The image of the Bundesbank tradition as invariably deflationary is a complete caricature. In any eight-year period you care to choose, Germany has had lower unemployment than Britain and the US, and usually faster productivity growth. This hardly suggests consistent deflation. And in any case, if we are eventually going to join the union, we should be in at the beginning, trying to affect its ethos. 'In delay there lies no plenty,' as Feste rightly sang.

Conclusion

So the economic reality is this. There are very many arguments for joining and one for staying out for ever. The argument for staying out will never go away, for a local shock could hit Britain just as well in fifty years' time as in five. So, if we are ever going to join, we should join now, while we can affect the design of the system and avoid the stigma of staying out.

It will carry little conviction if we say that we plan to join in five years' time. For there is a tide in the affairs of men. The tide appears to be running strongly. Now is the time to show our colours.

There is of course a major political dimension to all this. The European movement is as much a movement to secure peace as to promote prosperity. Some people think that the danger of war between civilised states has gone. So thought Norman Angell in 1910. But to understand the fifty years of peace in Europe since 1945, we should never forget the influence of the threat from Russia. That is now gone, and Chancellor Kohl has reason to fear the return of the old rivalries. Moreover Europe has a huge potential role as a peacekeeper outside Europe. These are the reasons why internationalists welcome greater international co-operation and European integration.

But the British people are, we know, ambivalent about these issues. They should not be pushed where they do not want to go. But they *should* be persuaded. The lead which politicians give is crucial.

The British people stand to gain immensely from European integration. They have a secret weapon – the English language. It is already the prime language of Europe, and it is fast becoming the language of the world. This is a growing asset, as more and more of the world's output becomes knowledge-based. English is the language of high-tech, be it air-traffic control or the Internet.

If Britain joins in the leadership of Europe, there will initially be three leaders – Germany, France and Britain. But the role of Britain will become increasingly important. London is already the New York of Europe, and Britain is the natural link between Europe and America. We shall gain immensely from our expanded European role.

By prolonging uncertainty over membership of EMU, the UK risks higher interest rates, exchange rate instability and higher inflation. Waiting brings few advantages but will add to internal division and uncertainty. The backlash will be on output and jobs.

What Labour Can Do

In early 1998 the UK will hold the European Union presidency. If the British are prepared to be bold and far-sighted, we can be midwives to the common currency. If not, we shall be covered in confusion.

That may not matter much. What will matter will be the confusion, which will last for years, about where we are going. It will consume our energies far more than a clear process of entry. If we care about jobs, let's take a lead in Europe rather than arguing endlessly.

The Labour Party has always been in principle an internationalist party. It recognises that the interests of Britain are best served by common endeavour with other countries, rather than by the solitary pursuit of British self-interest. A natural expression of that faith would be to join the single currency.

Joining Europe's Currency

Summary

- *There are strong economic arguments for joining the European single currency, listed in Table 18. There would also be one major risk.*

- *The main advantages for Britain would be lower inflation, lower interest rates, no exchange rate uncertainties within Europe, and a more stable monetary policy than in the past. In addition we should avoid the risk of losing out in Europe through failing to join the club.*

- *The disadvantage of abandoning a flexible exchange rate is that we are then less able to offset a large shock that affects Britain but not our neighbours. We could still however use the budget to stabilise our economy, provided we negotiate with our partners for reasonable national autonomy over budgets.*

- *Almost certainly we shall eventually join. If so, there is every reason to be in at the start in order to influence the rules and procedures that are adopted. If we dither instead, we shall waste time in fruitless internal debate and division.*

- *If Britain became a whole-hearted member of the European Union, it would increase its influence in the world. The English language would give Britain a key role in Europe and would give us the moral strength to challenge many of the worse features of current EU policy and practice. That would enhance prosperity in Europe and in Britain.*

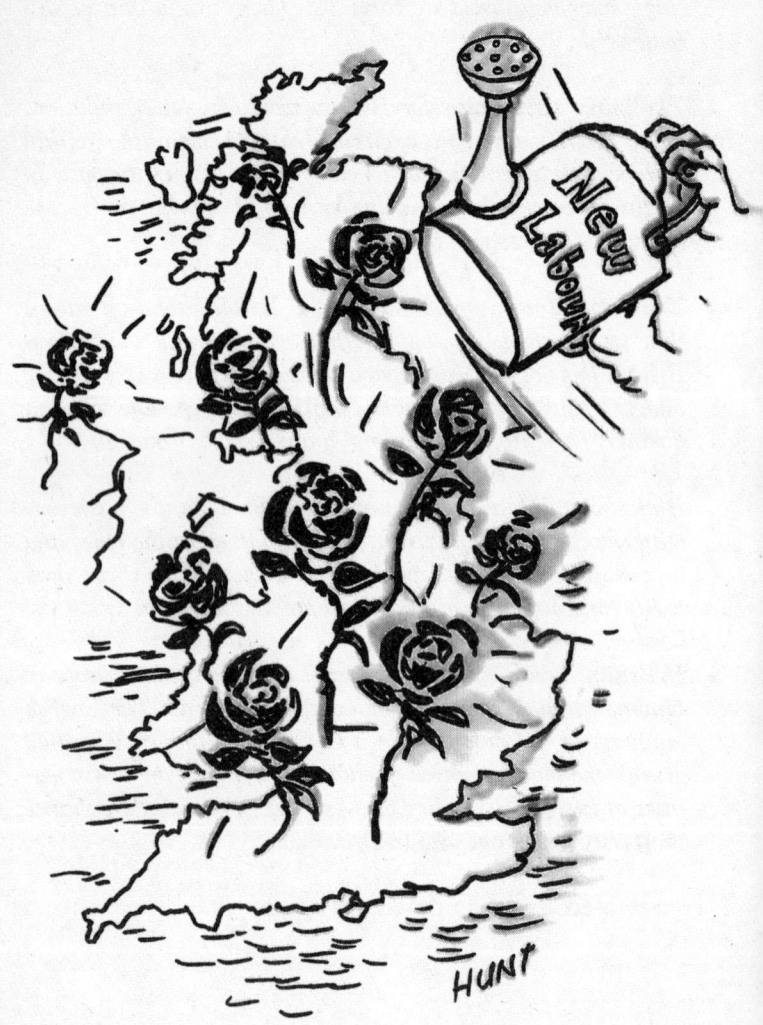

9

Can Labour Do It?

Equality of opportunity should not be a one-off, pass-fail, life-defining event – but a continuing opportunity for everyone to realise their potential.

Gordon Brown[1]

IN THIS BOOK I have said what I believe Labour *should* do. The key aim has been to describe policies which would actually work. Much needs doing, and I have summarised it at the end of each chapter. The top priorities are these:

EDUCATION
- numeracy and literacy for everyone by the age of eleven
- a skill for everyone by the age of eighteen, with everyone studying to at least Level 2
- increased spending on education (and health) relative to GDP

EMPLOYMENT
- prevent long-term unemployment through guaranteed offers of work
- better child-care to help mothers work

INEQUALITY
- a rising minimum income for pensioners but a phased-in requirement to save for a second-tier pension

COMPANIES
- prohibit price-rigging and anti-competitive behaviour
- discourage inefficient takeovers, improve corporate governance, and support small business

ECONOMIC STABILITY
- avoid boom and bust through better financial policy and more consensus about wages

EUROPE
- join the single currency

WHAT CAN WE EXPECT FROM LABOUR?

But what will a Labour government actually do? Will it make a difference? After all, governments have limited power, and limited room for manoeuvre. In peacetime at least, people have a limited tolerance for change. Tax revenue will remain in short supply, and most changes will have to be financed from existing resources.

Even so, governments do make a huge difference. They alter the priorities of public spending, they alter the way the government operates, and they alter the atmosphere in the country as a whole – by changing what is valued and what is not. As evidence you have only to think about the last eighteen years. So what can we actually expect from Labour?

LABOUR'S PROMISES

Some people say that Labour has few explicit policies. That is simply untrue. Labour has produced well thought-out policies, set out in well-reasoned policy documents.[2] If these were implemented, they would make an enormous difference.

To see this, let me list Labour's main specific commitments which have a bearing on our economic performance.[3]

EDUCATION
- a nursery place available for every child aged four
- no classes of over thirty for children aged 5–7
- every youngster under eighteen enrolled for a Level 2 qualification or above (Target 2000)
- a University for Industry, making distance learning available for all
- a General Teaching Council to raise teacher standards
- Learn As You Earn accounts to help adult learning
- education spending to rise faster than GDP

EMPLOYMENT
- for under twenty-fives, no unemployment beyond six months (reducing unemployment by 250,000)
- for all people unemployed over two years, a recruitment subsidy of £75 a week for six months
- a new personal development and guidance service for everyone aged 14–18
- welfare spending to rise slower than GDP as a result of back-to-work policies

INEQUALITY
- a national minimum wage
- more house-building by local authorities to combat homelessness

COMPANIES
- prohibition of anti-competitive practices
- large firms to pay interest on overdue debt
- regional development agencies to encourage local small businesses

ECONOMIC STABILITY
- over the cycle, no rise in public debt relative to GDP, nor borrowing to finance public consumption
- Bank of England procedures reformed to reduce the personal factor in monetary policy

EUROPE
- sign the Social Chapter
- closer co-ordination of economic policy through the Council of Ministers as a political counterpart to the proposed European Central Bank

This in itself is a formidable list of commitments. If a government did all this, it would make a huge difference. Imagine a world where youth unemployment had been halved and every youngster got a worthwhile skill.

Tony Blair has asked to be judged by whether he delivers these promises – and he will be.[4] Over time new commitments will also emerge: no sensible party promises in opposition all that it hopes to achieve if elected, so hopefully Labour will achieve even more in government than it currently promises.

LABOUR'S PHILOSOPHY

But for most voters what matters today is not the detail of policy but how they perceive Labour's general attitudes and competence. In terms of calibre and competence the Labour team is a clear match for the existing government. So the choice does in the end come down to what kind of country you want. What attitudes should underpin our affairs?

For eighteen years the present government has stressed the role of self-interest as *the* engine of progress. It is of course a potent force and it must be used, but two major problems arise if you elevate self-interest above all other principles.

Self-interest works well for those who have the means to

pursue it. But many people do not – unless we empower them. Everyone has to get a skill and everyone has to receive help when their luck turns sour. It is the job of society to empower people: to help them to help themselves.

The policy of empowerment must cover everybody. In the last eighteen years more and more people have become powerless. More people sleep on the streets, while the rich get richer and richer. Labour's stated aim is to stop this growing inequality, and to re-order society in the interests of the many, not the few. To illustrate the point, Labour wants to lower the starting rate of tax, which affects everyone, while the Conservatives want to abolish the taxes on capital gains and inheritance, which affect the few. As Tony Blair has put it: 'One Britain. That is the patriotism for the future. Where your child in distress is my child; your parent ill and in pain is my parent; your friend unemployed or helpless, my friend; your neighbour, my neighbour.'[5]

And there is another problem with unbridled self-interest. It does not bring satisfaction, even to those who succeed. It leads to envy, bad treatment of colleagues, and insecurity. Increasingly the assumption is that everyone is self-serving and that no one can be trusted. Professions which used to work from a motive of service are forced into artificial forms of competition. And in the business world, standards of behaviour deteriorate. As a result, many people are not satisfied even with fat pay-cheques, because they are stressed out worrying about office politics.

This kind of turmoil is not mainly the result of international competition – that is a force which limits our options but cannot possibly dictate our responses. In fact we can deal with international competition better if we build solid, far-sighted companies based on trust than if we dump our colleagues at the first whiff of difficulty. So, even among the privileged, mutual help must be a basic principle, beside self-interest. This is what Labour stands for.

We want a government that is committed to including

everyone, so that everyone can make the most of their potential in an atmosphere of mutual respect. Society must be inclusive; it must be empowering; and it must generate contentment.

But society must also be dynamic. Britain has a huge advantage in the knowledge-based industries, where English is the *lingua franca* throughout the world, and we have an excellent system of higher education. So we are well placed to be leaders in the information technology world of the future. But we shall never succeed unless we can involve everybody in this endeavour. The information superhighway has the wonderful power to reach every classroom and every work place, and Labour has pledged to do just that.

Labour's stated objective is to produce a more cohesive society in which everyone can make a contribution and everyone receive a proper share. For a Labour government the acid test will be this: do more people get more out of their lives?

Labour can surely meet that test.

Notes

PREFACE

1. *Centrepiece* (three issues a year), Centre for Economic Performance, London School of Economics (fax: 0171 955 7595).
2. Commission on Public Policy and British Business, *Promoting Prosperity: A Business Agenda for Britain*.

CHAPTER 1: WHICH WAY BRITAIN?

1. The evidence is in Chapter 2 onwards.
2. Some people have used the word in a wider sense, implying renewed power for workers' organisations at the workplace. I am not using the word in that sense.
3. Among the seven biggest recessions we also find the UK recession of 1973–75 (a 3.4% fall in GDP).

CHAPTER 2: THE KEYS TO SUCCESS

1. The figures relate to output per hour worked. If instead we focus on output per person employed, the figures for

1979–96 are (% per year): US, 0.9; W. Germany, 1.6; France, 1.7; UK, 1.8. For 1988–96 the figures are: US, 0.9; W. Germany, 1.9; France, 1.5; UK, 1.5. For the *level* of output per hour see footnote 7 below.

2. From 1979 to 1995 growth in manufacturing output was: Britain, 13%; Germany, 20%; Spain, 24%; Italy, 25%; Netherlands, 33%; Sweden, 33%; Japan, 49%; USA, 55%; France, 6% (OECD data).

3. See Goodman and Webb (1995), Table 3. The 'top 5%' in the text means the 95th percentile of individuals, and the 'bottom 5%' means the 5th percentile – ranked on the basis of real expenditure per adult-equivalent within the household.

4. The most reliable comparisons of inequality in living standards are in Atkinson, Rainwater and Smeeding (1995). The figures of inequality given in the World Bank's *World Development Report* and reprinted in the UNDP *Human Development Report* exaggerate Britain's inequality. (They relate to the distribution of household income across households, whatever the size of the household.)

5. Due to increased inequality of pre-tax incomes, the share of taxes paid by the rich has risen. But even so, the relative post-tax incomes of the rich have risen hugely.

6. The population of working age is growing faster in the US than in Europe, so that total output growth is similar in the US and Europe. The rate of return on capital is also high in the US, but this is the natural result of underinvestment.

7. Hours from OECD *Employment Outlook*, 1996, where UK data correspond to the LFS. For US we used a figure of 1850 hours (on the advice of R. Freeman). On this basis hourly productivity at PPP exchange rates in 1995 was (US=100): Canada, 85; Japan, 65; France, 106; western Germany, 110; UK, 82. For Belgium, Netherlands and Italy see Pilat (1996).

8. Between 1979 and 1993 real hourly earnings of the

bottom decile fell by 20% for US white males, and they rose by 14% in Britain (Current Population Survey and New Earnings Survey).
9. The difference between the USA and Europe is less if we focus on total non-employment rather than simply the unemployment of those seeking work. For males aged 25–54 in 1988–94 the non-employment rate (%) was: US, 11.8; France, 11.4; UK, 13.4; western Germany, 14.6.
10. Freeman (1996). (Data relate to male population of working age.) Those in jail are not included in the civilian labour force; including them might raise the US non-employment rate in the previous footnote by around one percentage point.
11. The OECD *Jobs Study* (1994) lavishes praise on the US labour market and urges US-style deregulation as a key element in the fight against unemployment. In my opinion we have gone far enough in this direction (see Chapters 3 and 4). Many observers have praised the so-called US jobs miracle. But this is mainly because the population of working age has been growing so much faster in the US, due to higher immigration and higher fertility.
12. International Assessment of Educational Progress, reported in Prais (1995).
13. See, for example, Barro and Sala-i-Martin (1995), Sachs and Warner (1995), Mankiw (1995), Ramey and Ramey (1995), Oulton (1995). Other important factors are high standards of health and low birth rates.
14. See Slemrod (1995). Barro and Sala-i-Martin (1995) find a negative effect of government consumption (excluding education, defence and transfer payments), but see comment in Chapter 5, footnote 2.
15. See, for example, Bruno, Ravallion and Squire (1995), Alesina and Rodrik (1994), Persson and Tabellini (1994), Birdsall, Ross and Sabot (1995).

16. For example, for given wage rates, high redistributive taxes distort work incentives, and, for given skills, high minimum wages cause unemployment.
17. Van Praag (1978), Layard and Glaister (1994, Chapter 5).
18. There is substantial evidence that it is mainly relative income which matters, and that at European income levels absolute income makes much less difference – see Clark and Oswald (1994), Kapteyn and Van Herwaarden (1980), Layard (1980).
19. See Fernie and Metcalf (1995).
20. For evidence on this paragraph and the next see Clark and Oswald (1994) on the cross-sectional effects of unemployment; Winkelman and Winkelman (1994) on the longitudinal effects of unemployment; and Blanchflower, Oswald and Warr (1993) on the effects of income and employment.
21. The extent of this distress is reflected in the movements of the suicide rate. In Britain this has fluctuated over the years with unemployment. There is also an underlying long-term upward trend in suicide for men, whose relative unemployment position has worsened, and a downward trend for women, whose relative unemployment position has improved (Oswald, 1995).
22. Freeman (1996), Chiricos (1987).

CHAPTER 3: A SKILLS REVOLUTION

1. The evidence is explored fully in Barro and Sala-i-Martin (1995).
2. In 1994 the actual figure not getting Level 2 by age 19–21 was 37%. Forty-three per cent got five Grade Cs at GCSE and another 20% got other qualifications (Department for Education Statistical Bulletin 7/94, July 1994, and National Advisory Council for Education and Training Targets [NACETT] Report on Progress, 1995).

Notes

3. Foxman *et al* (1993). Numeracy fell between 1964 and 1983 (Reynolds and Farrell, 1996).
4. Prais (1995).
5. That is, National Curriculum Level 4.
6. National Commission on Education (1993), Sylva and Moss (1993).
7. Mortimore and Blatchford (1993).
8. In the UK in 1994–95 pupils per teacher were: primary, 21.6; secondary, 15.9 (DfEE *Educational Statistics in the UK*). In England FTE students per teachers were: further education, 15.4 (1994–95); higher education, 16.5 (1993–94) (DfEE *Departmental Report*, 1996, pp. 184–5).
9. National Foundation for Educational Research estimate. Labour is proposing to meet this cost by abolishing the Assisted Places Scheme which subsidises 30,000 children in independent schools.
10. For a fuller discussion of these issues (and a slightly different and earlier proposal) see Layard, Robinson and Steedman (1995).
11. *Labour Force Survey*.
12. DfEE (1996) – target for Level 2 key skills. The Dearing Report (1996) recommends that all publicly-funded trainees aged 16–19 should study the key skills.
13. They would normally study for a GNVQ – see below – which includes maths and other requirements from which they would be exempted if they got the relevant GCSEs.
14. For more information on NVQ and GNVQ see Robinson (1996).
15. The existing NACETT target for Level 3 is 60% by the year 2000. This is a sensible target.
16. If you are under nineteen on 31 August in the calendar year when your course starts, your education on that course is free.
17. This does not include fees paid by TECs or local authorities from public funds.
18. Angrist and Krueger (1991), Angrist and Krueger

(1992), Ashenfelter and Krueger (1994), Ashenfelter and Rouse (1996).
19. See Barr (1989).
20. I assume a real interest rate of 4%. For earnings I use the current cross-sectional earnings profile of graduates augmented by 2% per annum real growth.
21. The loan would not count within the PSBR provided the risk was privately borne. The private sector would also pay the Inland Revenue an agency fee for acting as debt-collector.
22. 1993–94 data. This includes the existing student loans scheme which, as a public sector loan, appears in government expenditure. (DfEE, *Educational Statistics in the UK*, 1995, p. 33.)
23. Op. cit. This is the public cost for British students only. It consists of the grant from the Higher Education Funding Council (£3.1 billion) plus students' fees paid by local education authorities (£1.8 billion).
24. Oxford and Cambridge get around £1,500 a year extra per student, because the government pays college fees as well as university fees. This anomaly should be eliminated.
25. CVCP, PES Submission 1996, October 1996.
26. This should include all courses leading to nationally recognised qualifications, but not recreational 'adult education' nor tailor-made courses put on at the request of individual firms.
27. Note that the savings account would only accumulate gradually, and would still be quite small by the age of, say, twenty-five. So it cannot help greatly to finance the key investments needed before then; its use comes later.
28. Higginson Committee (1988).

CHAPTER 4: FROM WELFARE TO WORK

1. Standard ILO definition of unemployment. The work-

Notes

force excludes people who choose not to be in paid work.
2. Each unemployed person costs the Exchequer something like £9,000 (data from Employment Policy Institute). The unemployed person also loses net income of something like £6,000, and firms lose post-tax profits of the order of £5,000 – making a total economic cost of around £20,000.
3. For evidence that long-term unemployment has little effect on inflation see Layard *et al* (1991, 1994).
4. For fuller analyses of the strategy proposed below see Layard (1995, 1996, 1997a, 1997b).
5. On Sweden see Layard and Philpott (1991) Chapter 4, and on Switzerland and Denmark see Schwanse (1995). See also OECD (1990).
6. See Jackman *et al* (1996). On other causes and non-causes of unemployment see pp. 73–7.
7. Layard (1997a). A similar proposal was made in Layard (1986) and proposed by the Employment Committee (1986). See also Employment Committee (1996) and the Right to Work Bill tabled by Ralph Howell, Frank Field and others, which however differs in important detail from the proposal in this chapter.
8. The worker would also get in-work benefits if eligible – see below.
9. For a good description of the kind of work that can be done see Simmonds and Emmerich (1996), which develops in some detail the idea of 'intermediate' forms of employment between unemployment and permanent jobs. An excellent example of such 'intermediate' employment is that provided by the WISE group in Glasgow.
10. Simmonds and Emmerich (1996) argue strongly for paying the rate for the job but, as they point out, this implies a gross cost per place of nearly £10,000 a year.
11. The existing long-term unemployed (the stock) are more difficult to help than those at the point of entering

long-term unemployment (the flow). To start on both at the same time might lead to failure, so it would be preferable if guarantees to the stock came into force a year after guarantees to the flow.
12. How fast depends on the response of the monetary authorities. If the monetary authorities have an inflation target, jobs will expand exactly in line with the increase in the effective labour supply.
13. See Layard (1986), Chapter 6.
14. In the short run there is some substitution and displacement, which then diminishes. In addition the benefit to each individual who is helped comes in part later.
15. Of people who left the unemployment claimant count in June 1995 and found work, 52% were back into unemployment within a year (*Labour Market Trends*, October 1996, p. 452). The best information on the jobs people get when they leave unemployment comes from the Labour Force Survey (data kindly provided by Paul Gregg). In 1994 those employees who were unemployed one year earlier had the following pattern of wages:

	Lower quartile	Median	Mean	Upper quartile
Weekly (£)	70.00	140.00	160.00	210.00
Hourly (£)	3.00	4.00	5.00	5.70

Those in employment who were unemployed one year earlier had the following pattern of activity when surveyed: permanent job, 58%; temporary job, 17%; self-employed, 13%; government scheme, 10%.
16. Machin (1996).
17. This is not true if you are an owner-occupier who has been unemployed for more than nine months. Your mortgage interest is then covered by Housing Benefit if you are unemployed, but not if you are in work. Among all those unemployed for more than nine months, 30% are paying

mortgages, 10% are outright owners, 43% are tenants of local authorities or housing associations and 17% private tenants. (Among all unemployed people the figures are 34, 11, 39 and 16%.)
18. But see previous footnote.
19. At present there is a system called Employment on Trial. If you quit a job between six and twelve weeks after leaving unemployment, you can go back on benefit even though you quit (if your previous spell of unemployment lasted over six months). The right is not well publicised, and six weeks may be too long an interval.
20. Benefit entitlement is calculated as follows. First calculate basic income (Job Seeker's Allowance if unemployed, or take-home pay if working). Then calculate Family Credit if working over sixteen hours a week. Then calculate Housing plus Council Tax Benefit. The withdrawal rates are 70% for Family Credit, 65% for Housing Benefit and 20% for Council Tax Benefit, but the iterative procedure should keep the maximum overall rate of withdrawal just below 100%. Notice that a cut in the starting rate (t) of income tax (and National Insurance) would do very little to reduce the overall withdrawal rate for those on the lowest incomes. For the highest overall rate of retention (or non-withdrawal) is $(1-t)(1-0.7)(1-0.65-0.2) = (1-t)(0.05)$. A cut in the starting rate would, however, reduce the number facing high withdrawal rates by lifting some people off means-tested benefit. If the starting rate of tax was reduced, the gains from this could be limited to the poorest families by simultaneously lowering the starting point of the standard rate band.
21. If only this is done, more families are brought on to benefit and thus on to high rates of withdrawal. But this can be avoided if lower band tax rates are cut at the same time (see previous footnote).
22. DSS (1996), p. 17. Take-up is 71% of eligible people and 81% of eligible money.

23. In principle, a more complete integration of taxes and benefits would be desirable. But, if benefits are to be targeted at the poor, they have to be related to family income and not individual income. The Inland Revenue currently only knows the income of a family (i.e., a couple) after the end of the tax year, which is far too late for the provision of poverty relief. A more radical approach is along the lines of a Basic Income Guarantee (BIG), which, it is supposed, would eliminate the need for means-testing. In its simplest form this would provide a sizeable grant to every person (or to every 'participant') and would then tax all income at a single tax rate, which would have to be high in order to cover the cost of the grant. The policy would involve a large increase in the marginal tax rate for most taxpayers. This is another form of means-testing (though less fraught with stigma because no claiming is involved) and it would introduce major disincentives for most taxpayers. The issue is really whether to have high marginal tax rates for all (as with BIG) or very high ones for a few, but lower ones for most (as now). On this debate see Piauchaud (1987) and Atkinson (1995b), Chapter 15, who favours a modified BIG (pp. 302–3).
24. Not in the public sector, where manual workers' pay was set by Whitley Councils, where employers and workers bargained under an independent chairman.
25. A Wages Board remains in the agricultural sector.
26. Dickens *et al* (1994a, b).
27. On the US see Card and Krueger (1995), and for an opposing view see Neumark and Wascher (1992). On Europe see Dolado *et al* (1996).
28. A minimum wage would also improve the public finances, through higher taxes and National Insurance contributions and lower in-work benefits. On the other hand, however, there would be a loss of Corporation Tax and an increased public sector pay-bill. These two effects might

roughly cancel each other out. (The benefit savings are small – around £150 for a minimum wage of £3.25 an hour. See IFS, *Options for 1997: The Green Budget*.)
29. For a survey of minimum pay issues see Fernie and Metcalf (1996) and IFS, *Options for 1997: The Green Budget*. As they explain, we ought to be wary of macro-economic-model-based arguments against minimum wages of the kind used by current government ministers, who sometimes forecast a million extra unemployed. The problem is primarily a microeconomic one and should be mainly assessed on that basis.
30. Wadsworth and Gregg (1995), p. 213, updated to 1997 earnings levels.
31. There is also a family premium of £10.55 which is paid if there are any children at all.
32. This benefit is for those who are sick for over six months, and the recruitment subsidy could begin a further six months after that. But reform here could not begin until the long-term unemployed programme was fully working.
33. Jackman *et al* (1996).
34. It would help employment if employers' taxes on low-wage workers were reduced, and those on high-wage workers increased (see Layard *et al*, 1991), as discussed earlier.
35. Layard (1986), pp. 178–9. An up-to-date repetition of this analysis by Tim Hughes yields very similar results.
36. OECD, *Jobs Study* (1994).
37. See Jackman *et al* (1996), and sources cited there.

CHAPTER 5: THE PROPER SIZE OF GOVERNMENT

1. There is of course an arbitrary element in the definition of public expenditure. For example, child support in Britain is through extra government expenditure, whereas in the US it is done through tax exemptions. The efficiency cost of each approach would be the same if the *marginal* rate of

tax was the same – even though the *average* rate (as measured) would be different.
2. See the thorough survey in Slemrod (1995) and, on welfare spending, the studies cited by Atkinson (1995a) Table 1. Barro and Sala-i-Martin (1995) find a negative effect of government exhaustive expenditure, excluding education and defence, but do not report on the effect of total government expenditure. (It is hard to see why expenditure on law and order, health, transport, etc., should be treated as having no investment dimension while defence and education have. It is also unclear why transfer payments are not considered a potential problem.) Fischer (1993) finds a negative effect of the budget deficit, but that is a different point – see Chapter 7.
3. Of course, if the relative cost of a service falls, it is possible to increase its consumption faster than GDP without it costing a higher share of money GDP. Unfortunately education and health are not like that. It is true that in some ways productivity grows rapidly in these sectors (for example knowledge accumulates), but what people want is contact with a teacher or doctor. The relative cost of such contacts rises with the real wage of teachers and doctors. So, if the number of staff is constant, the share of education and health in GDP is constant, and if there is an increase in staff the share rises. Discontent with NHS waiting lists directly affects the level of private health insurance, but this still covers only around 15% of the population.
4. Between 1992 and 2001 the number of people over state pension age in the UK is forecast to increase by 220,000, and the number of children under sixteen by 550,000 (OPCS, National Population Projections, 1992).
5. For useful discussions see Flemming and Oppenheimer (1996) and Robinson (1993).
6. We could of course cut public expenditure and taxes at a stroke if we called pensions 'tax rebates' – given in return

Notes

for previous taxes paid. But this would be mere sleight-of-hand, since there are major redistributive features within the pension system: people with low lifetime incomes gain and those with higher lifetime incomes are net contributors.

7. The time may indeed come when Child Benefit should be taxed.
8. In fact they are worse in terms of tax exemptions than in terms of expenditures.
9. There is of course 'creep' in the standards the public expects. But that is a proper feature of higher income levels.
10. In most European countries the share has risen since 1979.
11. Another constraint which is often proposed is the so-called golden rule – that the government can borrow to cover *capital* expenditure (since this gives a future yield), but not to cover *current* expenditure. If we take the normal definition of capital expenditure, which covers fixed expenditure on buildings, roads and the like, this now amounts to around 1% of GDP (when it is measured net of depreciation). However, other expenditures (like much of education and health) also yield future returns, some of which increase government revenue, while some 'capital' expenditures (on, say, cultural facilities) do not. Thus a more comprehensive approach makes sense. The stable debt: income ratio is based on the idea that it is all right to borrow, provided government and private investments are raising the tax base in line with the debt. There is of course no rationale whatsoever for the idea of a zero budget balance (i.e., a budget balanced over the cycle) – which would imply a steadily vanishing debt: income ratio. Why should a government, any more than a firm, have no debt?
12. HM Treasury, *Financial Statement and Budget Report*, 1997–98. The government expenditure forecasts are

usually underestimates – see Goldman Sachs, *UK Economics Analyst*. The figures relate to the government's target measure, which is called general government expenditure ignoring privatisation (GGE[X]).

13. For the years up to 2000, current plans allow for very little increase in real government expenditure.
14. Pay accounts for a quarter of public expenditure, so a 2% increase in real pay increases real public expenditure by ½%.
15. The simplest way would be to raise the real tax threshold or the lower rate of tax, and also lower the real threshold at which the standard rate of tax begins.
16. Hewitt (1989).
17. Crooks (1989).
18. Another possible tax would be a specific health tax, focused on taxpayers with above average incomes and used to finance the NHS.
19. They have also arranged to raise the retirement age of women from sixty to sixty-five, over the period 2010 to 2020.
20. This would cost an extra £700 million a year by the end of a five-year Parliament. For a related proposal see Commission on Social Justice (1994).
21. For evidence on inequality among pensioners see Johnson and Stears (1995).
22. For related proposals see Field (1995, 1996) and Dilnot *et al* (1994).
23. For a simple explanation of how this works in a closed economy see Atkinson (1995a). In an open economy, national saving has a weaker effect on domestic investment and thus output growth, but it still has a strong effect on income (including the returns on our investments abroad).
24. *Social Security Departmental Report*, March 1996, p. 41.
25. For a discussion see Field (1995, 1996) and Richards (1996).

26. It is sometimes said that, to allow for this, the PSBR should be set equal to capital expenditure net of depreciation. The idea here is that all current outlays plus the debt service on previous capital expenditure should be financed by current taxes. This would in effect exempt all present capital expenditure from the PSBR constraint. The difficulty with this approach is that it would soon lead to an argument about which elements of education, health, etc., constituted investments. It is therefore better to stick to the fundamental idea that the debt:income ratio must not explode. This idea should, however, never be allowed to prevent the undertaking of a worthwhile project. This means that *either* temporary aberrations of the debt:income ratio are accepted when clearly justified, *or* taxes are varied appropriately, *or* both.

27. Under a top-up voucher, if all voters had one child and taxes were proportional, the voter with average income would be indifferent to the level of £x. But the median voter, who has less than average income, would prefer a higher £x. However, once we recognise that people have different numbers of children, we reach a situation where the median voter would prefer a lower £x.

CHAPTER 6: LONG-TERM GROWTH – NOT SHORT-TERM PROFIT

1. The whole analysis in this chapter is heavily influenced by discussions with colleagues in the Commission on Public Policy and British Business – see its report (1997), Chapters 3, 4 and 5. For a good analysis of the short-termism debate see Nickell (1995) and Bond and Jenkinson (1996). See also Kay and Silbertson (1995), Hutton (1995), Milner ed. (1996), Westall ed. (1996) and Kay (1996).

2. The government has attempted to conceal this simple truth by focusing on investment 'in the business sector'

(DTI, 1996). But privatisation makes the definition of the business sector different in every country. Moreover, to explain economic growth, we should certainly include infrastructure investment as well. (There is of course a case for excluding housing investment, but even if we did exclude it Britain would still be last in Table 14.)
3. Real gross domestic fixed capital formation is still well below its level in 1988–90.
4. For a good survey of private and social rates of return to research and development see Cameron (1996), Table 3.
5. See Wardlow (1994). He reports a Bank of England survey of 250 industrial firms, mostly large and medium-sized. He also mentions that the use of the pay-back period was particularly common among smaller companies.
6. Mayer in Westall ed. (1996).
7. In Britain there are fund managers who often control substantial blocks of shares in a company. But their incentives are not long-termist, since they themselves are often assessed (by the funds they manage) on the basis of their own quarterly performance.
8. Britain also has a high dividend payout ratio (Hutton, 1995, p. 160.) This is said to be because institutional investors require it, but it is unclear why they would not be just as happy to have higher re-investment rates and higher capital gains, financing their clients' needs from capital disposals as well as from dividends. Moreover it is not clear whether high dividend payout causes or reflects low investment. It is also interesting that more investment in Britain than elsewhere is financed from abroad, and more British funds flow abroad.
9. In 1984–88, takeovers accounted for 3.2% per year of the capital stock of the corporate sector in Britain (Franks and Mayer, 1990). About half of takeovers by value were contested.
10. For evidence that having a large owner improves productivity growth, see Nickell *et al* (1997).

Notes

11. Royal Society of Arts (1995).
12. *Financial Times*, 7 November 1995.
13. Kay and Silbertson (1995).
14. Abell and Khalif (1996). The diversification is of no value to the shareholders, since they could have done it anyway through the stock market. It is also of no value to the bulk of workers, except in so far as cross-substitution is used to pursue stakeholder objectives.
15. Franks and Mayer (1992). The shareholders of the company which is taken over do however gain on average, due to a rise in their share price.
16. There is no evidence that the productivity or other performance indicators of taken-over companies improve on average after the takeover. This is true for agreed mergers and hostile takeovers alike.
17. A different bankruptcy code (nearer to the US model) would also lead to more firms continuing as going concerns.
18. Cadbury Committee (1992). The Committee was set up by the Financial Reporting Council, the London stock exchange and the accountancy profession.
19. *The Myners Report* on investor–company relations adopts the same point of view. This Working Group was set up with encouragement from the DTI.
20. The average period for which a share is held by the same shareholder is roughly three years; the average period for which a job is held is roughly four years.
21. Companies covered are those with over 1,000 employees in total, and over 150 in each of two countries.
22. See for example Fernie and Metcalf (1995).
23. They do not go as far as some would like. For example Kay and Silbertson (1995) dispute the idea of shareholders as owners, and wish to have chief executives appointed by a committee not answerable to the shareholders. They propose that the firm should maximise the total economic rent of shareholders and workers. This

implies normal rules for investment and employment, but these would be difficult to apply if workers were in fact getting *more* than the outside wage (workers would have the same type of incentive to restrict employment as workers in a self-managed Yugoslav enterprise). Supernormal wages also encourage unemployment. Where Kay is right is in denouncing a focus on short-term return on equity (i.e., dividend plus change in share price) as opposed to post-tax earnings per share over a longish time period.
24. On this section, see Nickell (1995, Chapter 4), Nickell *et al* (1997), and Aaronson (1996).
25. See Porter (1990) and previous footnote.
26. This would help to reduce the triplicate work now done on each case (at OFT, MMC and the DTI). Instead the OFT would do the main work.
27. Storey (1994), Chapter 4.
28. This is a better approach than establishing a new set of regional development banks.

Chapter 7: No More Boom and Bust

1. One can look at annual growth rates and then take their standard deviation. For 1979–95 the figures are (%): UK, 2.3; US, 2.0; western Germany, 1.9; Japan, 1.8; Italy, 1.4; France, 1.3.
2. For a large country the mix of monetary and fiscal policy also affects real interest rates and thus the long-run growth of output.
3. Using standard ILO definition of unemployment – see *Labour Market Trends*, September 1996, Table 7.3.
4. An alternative target – for the level of nominal GDP – has been proposed by a number of people including James Tobin, James Meade and Samuel Brittan. Nominal GDP equals the price level times the level of output. What difference does this make? If the economy is subjected to a

'demand shock', prices and output move together; so a policy to stabilise prices will also stabilise output and thus nominal GDP. There is no special advantage in focusing on nominal GDP rather than prices. But if the economy is subjected to a 'supply shock', prices and output move in opposite directions. For example, if prices rise, output will fall. With an inflation target it would then be necessary to engineer a further fall in output in order to reduce prices. This would be less necessary with a nominal GDP target, since nominal GDP had already been reduced by the fall in output. However, a similar response to such a supply shock can in fact be achieved if we have an inflation target consisting of a band where we are, normally, in the middle. If there is a shock, we can then let inflation rise somewhat in order to avoid an excessive immediate squeeze on output. Proponents of a nominal GDP target often talk as though nominal GDP is easier to control than inflation. But in the short run this is not the case, since both prices and output are in their own way difficult to forecast.
5. For a rigorous explanation of the 'time-inconsistency problem' see Barro and Gordon (1983).
6. There is of course a problem of interpretation, since countries that are most averse to inflation may have chosen to have independent central banks.
7. A rule which has become increasingly popular for setting interest rates is the Taylor rule, which holds that nominal interest rates should equal (i) the long-run target real interest rate plus (ii) the long-run target inflation plus (iii) half the excess of output over the sustainable level plus (iv) half the excess of inflation over the long-run target level. See for example Gavyn Davies *et al.* in Goldman Sachs, *The International Economics Analyst*, June 1996.
8. For a fuller discussion see Chapter 5, footnote 11.
9. This is our government debt minus the debts owed to the government.

10. HM Treasury, *Financial Statement and Budget Report*, 1997–98, p. 17.
11. For further discussion see Layard (1990).

CHAPTER 8: JOINING EUROPE'S CURRENCY

1. For a fuller discussion of the case for entry see Johnson (1996). For the case against see Connolly (1995). For an agnostic view see Bean (1992).
2. Those voting would be the governors of each national central bank plus six board members of the European Central Bank. (The model here is that of the Bundesbank and their regional central banks.) Interest rates would be decided by simple unweighted voting – where each individual was meant to vote for the European interest.
3. The exact phrase is that, 'The member state has respected the normal operating margins provided for by the Exchange Rate Mechanism of the EMS without severe tensions for at least two years.' These margins are now very wide (±15%), but we are not in the ERM. A further criterion is that our central bank is independent; this could be enacted after the general election.
4. The exchange rates with the yen and US dollar would continue to fluctuate. But more than half our trade is with Europe. This outweighs the point that the D-Mark tends to fluctuate more against the dollar than the pound does.
5. For further discussion see *Report of the City Research Project* (Corporation of London, 1995). The international wholesale functions of the City now employ some 150,000 people and generate an output of £10–15 billion. One risk is that the TARGET method of settling payments in Europe might be more costly to non-members of the club.
6. If the single currency succeeds in producing more market

Notes

   integration, then greater differences may occur. But this will reflect the success of the programme.
7. In many states the state has its own rules limiting deficits. But these were introduced for local reasons – not to protect other states against an irresponsible neighbour (Eichengreen and Von Hagen, 1995).
8. It is easier to see the reasons for the limits on debt than on deficits, and putting some pressure on high-debt countries (like Italy) is no bad idea.
9. Many European countries, unlike Britain, have big looming deficits due to excessive future pension liabilities.

CHAPTER 9: CAN LABOUR DO IT?

1. From 'New Labour and Equality', Second John Smith Memorial Lecture.
2. The main documents are listed on pp. 177–8.
3. Three of these items are among Labour's 'Five Early Pledges' (on primary school classes, youth unemployment, responsible budgets, hospital waiting lists and speedy trial for young offenders). A further three of the items were highlighted in Tony Blair's Ten Pledges in his 1996 conference speech – the pledges on education spending, welfare spending and Europe.
4. Labour also of course has huge legislative commitments on constitutional reform – devolution, electoral reform and the House of Lords – as well as pledges for action on crime and the NHS.
5. Blair (1996), p. 71. His 1995 conference speech.
6. A survey by the Institute of Management of 1,100 managers showed that half did not look forward to going to work. The two most stressful work issues reported were office politics and unreasonable deadlines. Comparison with a similar previous survey shows that stress increased between 1993 and 1996.

Labour Party Policy Documents

General
'New Labour: New Life for Britain'

Education
'Diversity and Excellence: A New Partnership for Schools'
'Excellence for Everyone: Labour's Crusade to Raise Standards'
'Aiming Higher: Labour's Plan for Reform of the 14–19 Curriculum'
'Labour's Plans for a Skills Revolution: Learn As You Earn'
'Lifelong Learning: Labour's Plans for Improving Access and Standards in Future and Higher Education, Adult and Continuing Education'
'Equipping Young People for the Future: Labour's Review of the Financing of Post-16 Education'

Welfare to Work
'New Labour: New Life for Young People'
'Getting Welfare to Work'

Public Expenditure
'New Partnerships for Investment: Labour's Approach to Public/Private Finance'

Companies
'Vision for Growth: A New Industrial Strategy for Britain'
'Labour and SMEs: The Growth Agenda'
'Building Prosperity: Flexibility, Efficiency and Fairness at Work'

Economic stability
'A New Economic Future for Britain'

Europe
'Business Agenda for Europe'
'The Future of the European Union'

All policies are summarised in the Party's *Policy Handbook*, and are available from:

The Labour Party, John Smith House, 150 Walworth Road, London SE17 1JT
Tel: 0171 701 1234, fax: 0171 277 3300
e-mail: labour-party@geo2.poptel.org.uk
Internet: http://www.poptel.org.uk/labour-party/
Public Information Line – tel: 0171 277 3346, fax: 0171 277 3555
Sales – tel: 0171 277 3389, fax: 0171 277 3339

References

SOURCES TO FIGURES

Figure 1

Growth rates are established as follows: OECD, *Economic Outlook*, December 1988, December 1995 and June 1996 (statistical annex, Tables 1 and 20). Except West Germany for 1988 to 1995, from *European Economy*, No. 60, 1995 (statistical annex, Tables 2 and 10). Except for West Germany, levels are established as follows: GDP at 1994 using current PPPs from OECD, *Economic Surveys UK* (at end) updated to 1996 prices by dollar inflation in the US; employment from OECD, *Economic Outlook*, June 1996 (statistical annex, Table 20). For West Germany, levels are established in 1987 by computing the French level in 1987 (as above) and getting the German level in 1987 as follows: we get GDP in 1987 for West Germany and France at 1987 PPP from OECD, *Economic Surveys UK* 1988–89 (at end) and employment for Germany and France from OECD, *Economic Outlook*. This gives us the ratio of Germany to France in 1987, and we apply this to the already computed French level in 1987.

Figure 2

Productivity is growth in output per person-hour, and is derived as follows. Firstly, GDP per employed person is obtained by subtracting the annual growth rate in employment from the annual growth rate in real GDP. To obtain the growth in output per person-hour we subtract the average annual growth rate in hours actually worked from the average annual growth rate in GDP per employed person. (Since there are no 1988 figures for average annual hours actually worked per person in employment, we use the available figures for 1983 and 1990 to obtain the 1988 figures by interpolation.) GDP and employment growth rates: OECD, *Economic Outlook*, December 1988, December 1995 and June 1996 (statistical annex, Tables 1 and 20). Except West Germany for 1988 to 1995, from *European Economy*, No. 60, 1995 (statistical annex, Tables 2 and 10). Hours: OECD, *Employment Outlook*, July 1996, p. 190.

Figure 3

OECD, *Economic Outlook*, December 1984 and December 1995 (statistical annex, Table 22). Unemployment standardised to ILO/OECD definitions.

Figure 4

OECD, *Economic Outlook*, December 1984, December 1995 and June 1996 (statistical annex, Table 22). Except West Germany (post 1991) and Europe (for all years) from *European Economy*, No. 60, 1995 (statistical annex, Table 3). Predictions for 1996 for all countries are obtained by chaining 'commonly used definition' unemployment rates from OECD, *Economic Outlook*, June 1996 (statistical annex, Table 21) to the above series. Europe is defined as EU 15 excluding East Germany. Unemployment standardised to ILO/OECD definitions.

References

Figure 5
Employment Policy Institute, *Employment Audit*, Issue One, June 1996. All data relate to the spring.

Figure 6
US: *Current Population Survey*, Britain: *New Earnings Survey*, Germany: *Socio-Economic Panel*.

Figure 7
Eurobarometer survey; see Oswald (1995), Table 3.

Figure 8
Clark and Oswald (1994) p. 648. Data originally from the British Household Panel Study's general health questionnaire (1991).

Figure 9
DfEE and Cabinet Office, *Skills Audit*, 1996, pp. 30, 40.

Figure 10
Third International Mathematics and Science Study (TIMSS), 1996.

Figure 11
DfEE and Cabinet Office, *Skills Audit*, 1996, p. 25.

Figure 12
Labour Market Trends, various issues. Compiled by following through cohorts of different initial duration over the following three months (in some cases, six or twelve months, adjusted *pro rata*).

Figure 13
Long-term unemployment: OECD, *Employment Outlook*, various issues. Benefit duration: Layard *et al* (1996).

Figure 14
OECD, *Economic Outlook*, June 1996 (statistical annex, Table 28). Projections for 1997.

Figure 15
Government expenditure: OECD, *Economic Outlook*, June 1996 (statistical annex, Table 28). Average for 1979–96. Real GDP growth: OECD, *Economic Outlook*, June 1996 (statistical annex, Table 1), except for W. Germany for 1988–95, from *European Economy*, No. 60, 1995 (statistical annex, Table 10). Population growth: OECD, *Labour Force Statistics*, 1995.

Figure 16
Hills (1995), Figure 4. Observations are for deciles of households averaged according to net income per adult-equivalent in the household.

Figure 17
The Penn World Tables (mark 5): an expanded set of International Comparisons, 1950–88, by Robert Summers and Alan Heston, *Quarterly Journal of Economics*, May 1991, non-residential capital stock per worker (1985 international prices).

Figure 18
OECD, STIU database, September 1996, Business Enterprise R&D expenditure as a percentage of GDP.

Figure 19
OECD, *Economic Outlook*, December 1988, December 1995 and June 1996 (statistical annex, Table 1).

Figure 20
OECD, *Economic Outlook*, June 1996 (statistical annex, Tables 14 and 22). Inflation is GDP deflator. Unemployment standardised to ILO/OECD definitions.

References

Figure 21
European Economy, No. 60, 1995 (statistical annex, Tables 26 and 53).

Figure 22
OECD, *Economic Outlook*, June 1996 (statistical annex, Tables 30 and 31).

SOURCES TO TABLES

Table 1
OECD, *Quarterly National Accounts* (volume indices of gross domestic product), No. 1, 1986; No. 1, 1992; No. 2, 1996. Size of recession measured by the percentage fall in GDP between quarterly peak and quarterly trough. Percentage fall = [(Volume index at peak) − (Volume index at trough)]/(Volume index at peak).

Table 2
OECD, *Employment Outlook*, 1996, Table 3.1, pp. 61, 62. The ratio of highest to lowest decile – for USA and UK: 1979 and 1995; Japan and France: 1979 and 1994; Sweden and West Germany: 1980 and 1993.

Table 3
Prais (1995).

Table 4
Eurobarometer survey; see Oswald (1995), Table 1 and Table 2. Data compares 1982–90 with 1973–81.

Table 5
Quarterly Labour Force Survey, spring 1995.

Table 6
J. Hills, *Joseph Rowntree Foundation Inquiry into Income and Wealth*, February 1995, Figures 3 and 7. Data for 1990–91.

Table 7
Social Security Departmental Report, March 1996, Cm 3213, p. 19. Data for 1995–96. Does not allow for costs of working (travel, clothes) nor free medical prescriptions when on benefit.

Table 8
Ibid, p. 20.

Table 9
Labour Force Survey, 1995. Wages have been updated to 1997.

Table 10
Dolado *et al* (1996), Table 1.

Table 11
Department of Social Security, *Social Security Statistics*, 1995, pp. 10, 21. Data for 1994. Includes only Income Support and Family Credit since most people on Housing Benefit and Council Tax Benefit also receive one of the first two benefits. (For unemployed people Income Support has now been replaced by Job Seeker's Allowance.)

Table 12
HM Treasury, *Public Expenditure: Statistical Analyses 1996–97*, Cm 3201, and *Social Security Departmental Report*, March 1996, p. 12. All figures except the breakdown of social security are from the Public Expenditure analyses. The breakdown of social security is given by the Social Security Departmental Report. The category 'sick' is an aggregation of 'long-term sick and disabled' and 'short-term sick'. The category 'widows and others' has been adjusted

so that the figure for total social security expenditure matches the figure given by the Public Expenditure analysis. Social Security includes Housing Benefit. Other includes: Trade/Industry/Energy (0.8), Agriculture (0.6), Overseas Representation and Aid (0.5), National Heritage (0.4), Debt interest (2.9), Miscellaneous – largely tax-collection and EC – (2.7).

Table 13
HM Treasury, *Public Expenditure: Statistical Analyses 1996–97*, Cm 3201, p. 11.

Table 14
Bond and Jenkinson (1996).

Table 15
Author.

Table 16
Porter (1990), Table 8.3.

Table 17
Storey (1995), Tables 2.6 and 2.7. Private sector workers. The European Commission defines the four categories of size as Micro, Small, Medium and Large.

Table 18
Author.

Table 19
Paul Krugman (1991), *Geography and Trade*, Cambridge, Mass.: MIT Press.

Bibliography

Aaronson, R. (1996), *The Future of UK Competition Policy*, London: Institute for Public Policy Research

Abell, P., and Khalif, H. (1996), 'Managerial Motives in the Market for Corporate Control', London School of Economics Centre for Economic Performance, mimeo

Alesina, A., and Rodrik, D. (1994), 'Distributive Politics and Economic Growth', *Quarterly Journal of Economics*, 109(2): 465–90

Angrist, J. D., and Krueger, A. B. (1991), 'Does Compulsory School Attendance Affect Schooling and Earnings?', *Quarterly Journal of Economics*, 106(4): 979–1014

――― (1992), 'Estimating the Payoff to Schooling Using the Vietnam-era Draft Lottery', National Bureau of Economic Research, Working Paper No. 4067

Ashenfelter, O., and Krueger, A. B. (1994), 'Estimates of the Economic Return to Schooling from a New Sample of Twins', *American Economic Review*, 84(5): 1157–73

Ashenfelter, O., and Rouse, C. (1996), 'Income, Schooling, and Ability: Evidence from a New Sample of Twins', NBER, mimeo

Atkinson, A. B. (1995a), 'The Welfare State and Economic Performance', Suntory-Toyota International Centre for Economics and Related Disciplines, Discussion Paper No. WSP/109.

――― (1995b), *Incomes and the Welfare State: Essays on Britain and Europe*, Cambridge: Cambridge University Press

Atkinson, A. B., Rainwater, L., and Smeeding, T. M. (1995), 'Income Distribution in European Countries' in Atkinson, A. B., *Incomes and the Welfare State: Essays on Britain and Europe*, Cambridge: Cambridge University Press

Barr, N. (1989), *Student Loans: The Next Steps*, Aberdeen: Aberdeen University Press

Barro, R. J., and Gordon, R. (1983), 'A Positive Theory of

References

Monetary Policy in a Natural Rate Model', *Journal of Political Economy*, 91(4): 589–93

Barro, R. J., and Sala-i-Martin, X. (1995), *Economic Growth*, New York: McGraw Hill

Bean, C. (1992), 'Economic and Monetary Union in Europe', *Journal of Economic Perspectives*, 6(4): 31–52

Bell, L., and Freeman, R. (1994), 'Why Do Americans and Germans Work Different Hours?', NBER, Working Paper No. 4808

Birdsall, N., Ross, D., and Sabot, R. (1995), 'Inequality and Growth Reconsidered: Lessons from East Asia', *The World Bank Economic Review*, 9(3): 477–508

Blair, T. (1996), *New Britain: My Vision of a Young Country*, London: Fourth Estate

Blanchflower, D. G., Oswald, A. J., and Warr, P. B. (1993), 'Well-being Over Time in Britain and the USA', London School of Economics Centre for Economic Performance, mimeo

Bond, S., and Jenkinson, T. (1996), 'The Assessment: Investment Performance and Policy', *Oxford Review of Economic Policy*, 12(2): 1–29

Bruno, M., Ravallion, M., and Squire, L. (1995), 'Equity and Growth in Developing Countries: Old and New Perspectives on the Policy Issues', World Bank Policy Research, Working Paper No. 1563

Cadbury Committee (1992), 'The Financial Aspects of Conflict Governance', London: Gee

Cameron, G. (1996), 'Innovation and Economic Growth', London School of Economics Centre for Economic Performance, Discussion Paper No. 277

Card, D., and Krueger, A. (1995), *Myth and Measurement: The New Economics of the Minimum Wage*, New Jersey: Princeton University Press

Centrepiece (thrice annual report), Centre for Economic Performance, London School of Economics (fax: 0171 955 7595)

Chiricos, T. (1987), 'Rates of Crime and Unemployment: An Analysis of Aggregate Research Evidence', *Social Problems*, 34(2): 187–211

Clark, A. E., and Oswald, A. J. (1994), 'Unhappiness and Unemployment', *Economic Journal*, 104(424): 648–59.

Commission on Public Policy and British Business (1997), *Promoting Prosperity: A Business Agenda for Britain*, London: Vintage

Commission on Social Justice (1994), *Social Justice: Strategies for National Renewal*, London: Vintage

Connolly, B. (1995), *The Rotten Heart of Europe*, London: Faber & Faber

Corporation of London (1995), *The Competitive Position of London's Financial Services*, Final Report of The City Research Project of the London Business School

Crooks, E. (1989), *Alcohol Consumption and Taxation*, London: The Institute for Fiscal Studies

Dearing, Sir R. (1996), *Review of Qualifications for 16–19 Year Olds*, Middlesex: SCAA Publications

Department for Education and Employment (DfEE), *Departmental Report* (1996), London: HMSO

Department of Trade and Industry (DTI) and Cabinet Office, (1996), 'The UK's Investment Performance: Fact and Fallacy', Competitiveness Occasional Paper

Dickens, R., Machin, S., and Manning, A. (1994a), 'The Effects of Minimum Wages on Employment: Theory and Evidence from Britain', London School of Economics Centre for Economic Performance, Discussion Paper No. 183

——— (1994b), 'Estimating the Effect of Minimum Wages on Employment from the Distribution of Wages: A Critical View', London School of Economics Centre for Economic Performance, Discussion Paper No. 203

Dickens, R., Machin, S., Manning, A., Metcalf, D., Wadsworth, J., and Woodland, S. (1995), 'Minimum Wages and UK Agriculture', *Journal of Agricultural Economics*, 46(1): 1–19

References

Dilnot, A., Disney, R., Johnson, P., and Whitehouse, E. (1994), *Pensions in the UK: An Economic Analysis*, London: The Institute for Fiscal Studies

Dolado, J., Kramarz, F., Machin, S., Manning, A., Margolis, D., and Teulings, C. (1996), 'The Economic Impact of Minimum Wages in Europe', *Economic Policy*, 23: 317–72

Eichengreen, B., and Von Hagen, J. (1995), 'Fiscal Policy and Monetary Union: Federalism, Fiscal Restrictions and the No-bailout Rule', Centre for Economic Policy Research, Discussion Paper No. 1247

Employment Committee (1986), *Special Employment Measures and the Long-term Unemployed*, London: HMSO

—— (1996), *The Right to Work/Workfare*, London: HMSO

Fay, R. (1995), 'Enhancing the Effectiveness of Active Labour Market Policies: The Role and Evidence from Programme Evaluations in OECD Countries', OECD, mimeo

Fernie, S., and Metcalf, D. (1995), 'Participation, Contingent Pay, Representation and Workplace Performance: Evidence from Britain', *British Journal of Industrial Relations*, 33(3): 379–416

—— (1996), 'Low Pay and Minimum Wages: The British Evidence', London School of Economics Centre for Economic Performance, Special Report

Field, F. (1995), *Making Welfare Work: Reconstructing Welfare for the Millennium*, London: Institute of Community Studies

—— (1996), *How to Pay for the Future: Building a Stakeholders' Society*, London: Institute of Community Studies

Fischer, S. (1993), 'The Role of Macroeconomic Factors in Growth', *Journal of Monetary Economics*, 32(3): 485–512

Flemming, J., and Oppenheimer, P. (1996), 'Are Government Spending and Taxes Too High (or Too Low)?', *National Institute Economic Review*, 3: 57–76

Foxman, D., Gorman, T., and Brooks, G. (1993), 'Standards of Literacy and Numeracy', in National Commission of Education, *Briefings*, London: Heinemann

Franks, J. R., and Mayer, C. (1990), 'Capital Markets and Corporate Control: A Study of France, Germany and the UK', *Economic Policy*, 10: 191–231

——— (1992), 'Hostile Takeovers in the UK and the Correction of Managerial Failure', Institute of Finance and Accounting, Working Paper No. 156–92, London Business School

Freeman, R. B. (1994), *Working Under Different Rules*, New York: Russell Sage Foundation

——— (1996), 'Why Do So Many Young American Men Commit Crimes and What Might We Do About It?', *Journal of Economic Perspectives*, 10(1): 25–42

Goodman, A., and Webb, S. (1995), 'The Distribution of UK Household Expenditure 1979–92', *The Institute for Fiscal Studies*, Commentary No. 49

Hewitt, P. (1989), *A Cleaner Faster London*, London: Institute for Public Policy Research

Higginson Committee (1988), *Advancing 'A' Levels*, London: HMSO

Hills, J. (1995), 'Funding the Welfare State', *Oxford Review of Economic Policy*, 11(3): 27–43

Hutton, W. (1995), *The State We're In*, London: Jonathan Cape

Jackman, R., Layard, R., and Nickell, S. (1996), 'Combatting Unemployment: Is Flexibility Enough?', London School of Economics Centre for Economic Performance, Discussion Paper No. 293

Johnson, C. (1996), *In With the EURO Out With the Pound*, London: Penguin Books

Johnson, P., and Stears, G. (1995), 'Pensioner Income Inequality', *Fiscal Studies*, 16(4): 69–94.

Kapteyn, S. M., and Van Herwaarden, F. G. (1980), 'Interdependent Welfare Functions and Optimal Income Distribution', *Journal of Public Economics*, 14(3): 375–97

Kay, J. (1996), *The Business of Economics*, Oxford: Oxford University Press

References

Kay, J., and Silbertson, A. (1995), 'Corporate Governance', *National Institute Economic Review*, 153: 84–97

Krugman, P. (1991), *Geography and Trade*, Cambridge, Mass.: MIT Press

Layard, R. (1980), 'Human Satisfactions and Public Policy', *Economic Journal*, 360(90): 737–50

—— (1986), *How to Beat Unemployment*, Oxford: Oxford University Press

—— (1990), *How to End Pay Leap-frogging*, London: Employment Institute

—— (1995), *Preventing Long-term Unemployment*, London: Employment Policy Institute

—— (1996), 'How to Cut Unemployment', *Centrepiece*, February

—— (1997a), *Preventing Long-term Unemployment: Strategy and Costing*, London: Employment Policy Institute

—— (1997b), 'Preventing Long-term Unemployment: An Economic Analysis', in Snower, D., and de la Dehesa, G. (eds.), *Unemployment Policy: Government Options for the Labour Market*, Cambridge: Cambridge University Press

Layard, R., and Glaister, S. (1994), *Cost-Benefit Analysis*, Cambridge: Cambridge University Press

Layard, R., Nickell, S., and Jackman, R. (1991), *Unemployment: Macroeconomic Performance and the Labour Market*, Oxford: Oxford University Press

—— (1994), *The Unemployment Crisis*, Oxford: Oxford University Press

Layard, R., and Philpott, J. (1991), *Stopping Unemployment*, London: Employment Institute

Layard, R., Robinson, P., and Steedman, H. (1995), 'Lifelong Learning', London School of Economics Centre for Economic Performance, Occasional Paper No. 9

Machin, S. (1996), 'Wage Inequality in the UK', *Oxford Review of Economic Policy*, 12(1): 47–64

Mandelson, P., and Liddle, R. (1996), *The Blair Revolution: Can Labour Deliver?* London: Faber & Faber

Mankiw, G. N. (1995), 'The Growth of Nations', *Brookings Papers on Economic Activity*, 1: 275–326.

Milner, S. (ed.) (1996), *Could Finance Do More For British Business?* London: Institute for Public Policy Research

Mortimore, P., and Blatchford, P. (1993), 'The Issue of Class Size', in National Commission on Education, *Briefings*, London: Heinemann

National Advisory Council for Education and Training Targets (NACETT), Report on Progress (1995)

National Commission on Education (1993), *Learning to Succeed*, London: Heinemann

Neumark, D., and Wascher, W. (1992), 'Employment Effects of Minimum and Sub-Minimum Wages: Panel Data on State Minimum Wage Laws', *Industrial and Labour Relations Review*, 46(1): 55–81

Nickell, S. (1995), *The Performance of Companies*, Oxford: Blackwell

Nickell, S., Nicolitsas, D., and Dryden, N. (1997), 'What Makes Firms Perform Well?', *European Economic Review*, vol. 41

OECD (1990), *Labour Market Policies for the 1990s*, Paris: OECD

——— (1994), *OECD Jobs Study*, Paris: OECD

Oswald, A. J. (1995), 'Happiness and Economic Performance', London School of Economics Centre for Economic Performance, mimeo

Oulton, N. (1995), 'Supply Side Reform and UK Economic Growth: What Happened to the Miracle?', *National Institute Economic Review*, 154: 53–70

Persson, T., and Tabellini, G. (1994), 'Is Inequality Harmful for Growth?', *American Economic Review*, 84(2): 600–21.

Piachaud, D. (1987), 'The Distribution of Income and Work', *Oxford Review of Economic Policy*, 3(3): 41–61.

Pilat, D. (1996), 'Labour Productivity Levels in OECD Countries: Estimates for Manufacturing and Selected

Service Sectors', OECD Economics Department, Working Paper No. 169
Porter, M. (1990), *The Competitive Advantage of Nations*, London: Macmillan
Prais, S. J. (1995), *Productivity, Education and Training*, Cambridge: Cambridge University Press
Ramey, R., and Ramey, V. A. (1995), 'Cross-country Evidence on the Link Between Volatility and Growth', *American Economic Review*, 85(5): 1138–59.
Reynolds, D., and Farrell, S. (1996), *Worlds Apart? A Review of International Surveys of Educational Achievement Involving England*, OFSTED Reviews of Research, London: HMSO
Richards, E. (1996), *Paying for Long-term Care*, London: Institute for Public Policy Research
Robinson, B. (1993), 'Britain's Borrowing Problem', Social Market Foundation Report No. 4
Robinson, P. (1996), 'Rhetoric and Reality: Britain's New Vocational Qualifications', London School of Economics Centre for Economic Performance, Special Report
RSA (1995), *Tomorrow's Company: The Role of Business in a Changing World*, London: Gower
Sachs, J. D., and Warner, A. (1995), 'Economic Reform and the Process of Global Integration', *Brookings Papers on Economic Activity*, 1: 1–118
Schwanse, P. (1995), 'The Effectiveness of Active Labour Market Policies: Some Lessons from the Experience of OECD Countries', paper presented to the OECD Technical Workshop in Vienna
Simmonds, D., and Emmerich, M. (1996), *Regeneration Through Work: Creating Jobs in the Social Economy*, Manchester: Centre for Local Economic Strategies
Slemrod, J. (1995), 'What Do Cross-country Studies Teach about Government Involvement, Prosperity, and Economic Growth?', *Brookings Papers on Economic Activity*, 2: 373–416
Storey, D. J. (1994), *Understanding the Small Business Sector*, London: Routledge

Sylva, K., and Moss, P. (1993), 'Learning Before School', in National Commission on Education, *Briefings*, London: Heinemann

Van Praag, B. M. (1978), 'The Perception of Income Inequality', in Krelle, W., and Shorrocks, A. (eds), *Personal Income Distribution*, Amsterdam: North Holland Publishing Company

Wadsworth, J., and Gregg, P. (1995), 'Making Work Pay', *New Economy*, 2(4): 210–13

Wardlow, A. (1994), 'Investment Appraisal Criteria and the Impact of Low Inflation', *Bank of England Quarterly Bulletin*, 34(3): 250–4

Westall, A. (ed.) (1996), *Competitiveness and Corporate Governance*, London: Institute for Public Policy Research

Winkelman, L., and Winkelman, R. (1994), 'Unemployment: Where Does it Hurt?', Dartmouth College, mimeo

Index

Page numbers in **bold** denote major section/chapter devoted to subject.

A-levels, 31; campaign for broader, **49–50**, 53
alcohol: taxes on, 89
apprenticeships, **40–3**
audit, efficiency, 110

Bank of England: and monetary policy, 126–7, 152
benefits: dependency on, 4; in-work, **65–7**, 68, 69, 78; unemployment, 64, 65–6, 78, 90
Beveridge, Sir William, 55
Blair, Tony, 152, 153
Britain: economic record, **12–16**; problems, 3–5; role in Europe, 7, 145, 147
budget, 122, 123, **127–8**, 131, 140, 147
Bundesbank, 126, 139, 143, 144

Cadbury Committee, 110, 111
California, 138
Calpers, 110
capitalism, British, **105–7**
Careers Service, 39, 52
'catch-up', 20, 21, 26, 102–3
CBI (Confederation of British Industry), 130, 131
Central Bank *see* European Central Bank
Chambers of Commerce, 115, 118
Child Benefit, 86
child-care, 72, 149
children: living on benefit, 71; lower-ability, 32–3
companies, **101–18**, 150, 153; characteristics of
    Anglo-American and German–Japanese, 105–7;
    competition policy, 112–14, 116, 118, 150;
    corporate governance, 110–11; deal-making culture,
    5, 107–8; encouragement of long-term growth, 6, 8,
    102, 108, 117; high turnover, 6, 15–16t;
    information disclosure to shareholders, 110, 117;
    Labour's commitments to, 151; objectives for
    reform, 108–9; and raising skills of employees,
    36–7, 41–2; and research and development, 104;
    short-termism of, 5, 13, 101–2, 104, 105–7, 117;
    takeovers, 105, 107, **109**, 110, 112–13, 117; worker
    participation, 111–12, 118; *see also* small firms
Companies Act, 106
competition policy, **112–14**, 116, 118, 150
contracts: and public services, **94–6**, 99
corporate governance, **110–11**
Council of Institutional Investors, 110, 111, 117, 118
Council of Ministers, 141, 144, 152
Council Tax Benefit, 65
crime, 4, 24; in United States, 18, 26

Index

Daimler-Benz, 107
Dearing Committee, 43
Dearing Report (1996), 50
defence: government expenditure, 87t, 90
downsizing, 5, 107, 108, 117

early retirement, 75
earnings: benefits related to, **65–7**, 68, 69, 78; of full-time employees, 43t; *see also* wages
Earnings Top-Up, 67
economy: factors contributing to growth, **20–2**; ineptness of macroeconomic management, 6–7; instability of, 119, 122f, **123–5**, 131, 136; and post-war recessions, 4, 5, 7, 24, 121, 125, 131, 136; problems with, 3–4; productivity record, 12–13, 26; sources of weakness, 4–5; stability of, 8, 150, 152
education, **29–53**; aim of raising minimum standards, 30, 37–40; apprenticeships, 40–3; campaign for broader A-levels, 49–50, 53; class size of primary schools, 34, 52, 151; companies and raising skills of employees, 36–7, 41–2; and Far East, 19–20, 26; financing of, 42, 43–6; government expenditure, 84t, 85, 87t; importance to economic growth, 19–20, 21, 26; Labour's commitments on, 151; as a lifelong process, 46–7; numeracy and literacy, 30, 31–3, 33–4, 40, 49, 52; nursery, 34, 52, 72, 79, 96, 97, 151; obtaining Level 2 qualification, 30, 31t, 37–9, 40, 41, 52, 151; record of qualifications, 30–3; reform of teaching profession, 34–6, 52; and school organisation, 36; technology of, 47–9, 53; and vouchers, 96–7
elderly: long-term care, 92–3, 99; *see also* pensions
Employee Share Ownership Plans *see* ESOPs
employees: participation in companies, 111–12, 118

employers: raising of skills of employees, 36–7, 41–2; rebates for hiring of unemployed, 59–60, 62, 63, 73, 78

employment, 149; importance of, 6, 55; insecurity of, 15–16, 24; Labour's commitments on, 151; protection of, 76; *see also* unemployment

Employment Service, 59, 72–3

empowerment, policy of, 153

EMU *see* single European currency

English (language), 45, 145, 147, 154

ERM (Exchange Rate Mechanism), 125, 134, 140

ESOPs (Employee Share Ownership Plans), 111–12

Euro, 134

Eurofighter, 90

Europe, **18–19**; and integration, 145; Labour's commitments on, 152; role of Britain in, 7, 145, 147; *see also* single European currency

European Central Bank, 127, 134, 135, 140, 143; and Council of Ministers, 141–2, 144, 152

European Commission, 74

European Union (EU), 146, 147; and Social Chapter, 76–7, 79, 111, 152

Exchange Rate Mechanism *see* ERM

exchange rates: and single currency, 135–6

expenditure, government, **81–99**, 127–8; categories, 84–6, 87t; and defence, 87t, 90; increase of above 40% of GDP, 98; international comparisons, 81–3; objectives, 83–4, 98; and pensions, 90–3, 97, 98–9; political pressure on increasing, 87; reducing of through Private Finance Initiative, 93–4, 99; social security, 85–6; taxes on anti-social activity, 88–90, 98; use of contracts in provision of public services, 94–6, 99; and vouchers, 96–7; and Windfall Tax, 88, 98, 128

Index

Family Credit, 65, 66, 67, 78
Far East, **19–20**, 26, 82, 83
Federal Reserve Board, 126, 138
Financial Management Certificate, 115, 118
France, 31, 105, 139, 140

GCSEs, 30
Geldard, Nicholas, 95
General Electric, 107
General Teaching Council, 35, 52, 151
Germany, 135, 142; and Bundesbank, 126, 139, 143, 144; commercial apprenticeship, 41; company approach, 19, 105–7; corporate governance, 111; economic approach, 18–19, 26; education, 30, 31; and ERM, 140; and pay consensus, 19, 26, 129; reunification, 18, 139–40; and small firms, 115; unemployment, 15, 19, 144
GNVQ2 (General National Vocational Qualification), 40
government expenditure *see* expenditure, government

health: government expenditure, 84, 85, 87t
Higginson Report (1988), 50
higher education, 29, 30; potential for rapid growth, 45–6; *see also* universities
housing, 151
Housing Benefit, 65, 66, 68

Incapacity Benefit, 73
Income Support, 71, 91
incomes *see* earnings; wages

Individual Learning Accounts, 42
industry associations, 41–2, 115–16, 118
inequality, 3, 4, 11, 16, 26, 90, 150; and crime, 24; disadvantage to growth, 6, 21, 26; Labour's commitment to stop, 151, 153; of wages, 13–14, 24, 55, 64
inflation, 123, 126, 142; short-term interest rates and, 124f; and single currency, 135; and unemployment, 57, 124f, 125, 128, 129
information, disclosure of, 110, 117
interest rates, 122, 123, 125; fluctuations in, 7, 121, 123, 125; inflation and short-term, 124f; and single currency, 135, 136, 140, 141
investment: and joining single currency, 136; low rate of, 102–4
in-work benefits, **65–7**, 68, 69, 78
Italy, 116

Japan, 82; and 'catch-up' process, 13, 19, 102–3; industries, 107, 112, 113t
Job Centre, 60, 61–2, 63, 66
Job Seeker's Allowance, 65, 66

Kohl, Chancellor Helmut, 145

Labour Party, 146; philosophy, **152–4**; policy commitments, **150–2**
Learn As You Earn accounts, 151
Learning Bank, 44–5, 47, 53
Level 2 qualification, 30, 31t, 40, 41, 151; changes

Index

needed to get youngsters up to standard of, 37–9, 52
lifelong learning, **46–7**, 53
literacy, 32, 33t, 52, 148
loans, student *see* student loans
long-term sick, 73
Low Pay Commission, 69

Maastricht treaty, 144; convergence criteria, 134
'macroeconomic' management, 6–7, 8
Major, John, 81
managers, 6, 12; in Germany, 19, 105; monitoring and accountability, 110–11; need to focus on 'organic growth', 102; and reform, 108; and short-termism, 102–3, 105; and takeovers, 107
manufacturing industry, 12
mathematics, 31–2, 50
mergers, 112–13; *see also* takeovers
minimum wages, **67–71**, 76, 78–9, 151
monetary policy, 122, 123, 125, **126–7**, 130, 131
Monopolies and Mergers Commission (MMC), 113
mothers, 71; proposals to help working, 6, 72, 79

National Economic Assessment, 129, 131
National Health Service *see* NHS
National Insurance contributions, 70–1, 74
National Insurance Fund, 92
National Vocational Qualification *see* NVQ2
NHS (National Health Service), 94–5
non-executive directors (NEDs), 111, 118

numeracy, 32, 33t, 52, 149

nursery education: need for universal provision, 34, 52, 72, 79, 151; vouchers, 34, 96, 97

NVQ2 (National Vocational Qualification), 30, 40

Office of Fair Trading (OFT), 113, 114

Open University, 48, 49

Organisation for Economic Co-operation and Development (OECD), 19, 58, 76

out-of-school activities, 72, 79

Patten, Chris, 82

pensions, 6, 14, 20, 86, **90–3**, 97, 98–9, 150

performance-related pay, 22, 27

petrol: taxes on, 89

PFI (Private Finance Initiative), **93–4**, 99

poor, 4, 55, 56t, 71

Prais, Sigmund, 32

primary schools: class size, 34, 52, 151; use of experienced 'helpers', 34

Private Finance Initiative *see* PFI

productivity, 12–13, 16, 26, 142

PSBR (public sector borrowing requirement), 94, 127

public expenditure *see* expenditure, government

public services: use of contracts and tendering in provision of, **94–6**, 99

rebates: for employers hiring unemployed, 59–60, 62, 63, 73, 78

recessions, post-war, 4, 5, 7, 24, 121, 125, 131, 136

Index

regional development agencies, 151
regional policy, 74
research and development (R & D), 46, 104
retirement, early, 75
Roach, Stephen, 108
'road pricing', 89
Robbins Committee, 47
Rome, Treaty of, 113–14, 118

satisfaction, 22–3, 26–7
schools, 29–30; class size of primary, 34, 52, 151; discipline, 24; organisation of, 36; studying for vocational qualifications at, 38–9
Schrempp, Jürgen, 107; quoted, 101
self-discipline, 20
self-interest, 152–3
SERPS (State Earnings Related Pension Scheme), 91
short-termism, 5, 13, 101–2, 104, 105–7, 117
sick, long-term, 73
Singapore, 31, 92
single European currency, 7, 8, 122, 127, **132–47**, 150; advantages, 135–7, 137t, 147; arguments against delayed entry, 142–5, 147; disadvantages, 137–40, 141, 142, 144; and ERM, 140; proposal, 133–4
skills: importance of, 5; need for improvement, 29–30; neglect of, 4, 21; *see also* education
small firms, **114–16**, 118, 151
smoking: taxes on, 89
Social Chapter, 76–7, 79, 111, 152
social security: government expenditure, 85, 87t, 90; role in redistributing income, 85–6
society: features of good, 25, 27

Society of Motor Manufacturers, 115–16
South Korea, 13
Speenhamland System, 68
stakeholder society: key steps towards, **5–6**
State Earnings Related Pension Scheme *see* SERPS
student loans, 43, 44–5, 47, 53
sub-degree education, 42, 46–7, 47–8, 52, 53
subsidies, 87

tables: advantages/disadvantages of joining single currency, 137; distribution of car production, 139; earnings, 14, 43, 70; 'effective marginal tax rates', 66; investment as percentage of GDP, 103; major rivals in Japanese industries, 113; minimum wages in other countries, 70; people living on means-tested benefits, 71; percentage reporting satisfaction with lives, 23; percentage of youngsters able to multiply, 20; poor, 56; public expenditure, 84, 87; ratio of out-of-work to in-work income, 65; recessions in G7 countries, 7; small firms, 114; types of firms, 106
takeovers, 105, 107, **109**, 110, 112–13, 117
Target 2000, 39, 52, 151; *see also* Level 2 qualification
taxes, 4, 14, 85, 98, 153; on anti-social activity, **88–90**, 98; effect on level of growth, 21; and Far East, 20; Windfall, 88, 98, 128
teaching profession: reform of, **34–6**, 52
'teaching schools', 35–6
technology: and education, **47–9**, 53
TECs (Training and Enterprise Councils), 115, 118
Thatcher, Margaret, 5, 11, 16, 21, 123
training: and employers, 36–7; teacher, 35–6; and unemployed, 60–1

Index

unemployment, 4, 6, 29, **56–7**, 122, 130, 131, 142–3; appraisal of other proposed remedies, 73–7, 79; and crime, 24; disadvantages of, 56; distress caused by, 6, 23, 24t, 27, 56, 57; evaluation of new schemes, 62–4; in Germany, 15, 19, 144; and inflation, 57, 124f, 125, 128, 129; job-creation projects, 60, 78; Labour's commitment to reducing, 151; and pay consensus, 129–30; prevention of long-term, 56–7, **58–62**, 78, 149; rebates for employers hiring, 59–60, 62, 63, 73, 78; rise in, 14–16, 55; training and, 60–1; in United States, 15f, 18, 26, 58

unemployment benefits, 64, 65–6, 78, 90

United States, **16–18**, 20, 22, 30, 31, 82, 105, 141; crime, 18, 26; Federal Reserve Board, 126, 138; health system, 84; inequality in, 13–14, 26; intellectual leadership, 45; minimum wage, 68; overvaluation of dollar, 136; and region-specific shocks, 138–9; unemployment, 15f, 18, 26, 58

universities, 50; finance, **43–6**; student loans, 43, 44–5, 47, 53

University for Industry, 48–9, 53, 151

vocational education, 38, 41; failure in, 29–30, 31–3; finance of, 42; NVQs, 30, 40; starting of at school, 38–9

vouchers, **96–7**, 99; nursery, 34, 96, 97

wages: consensual approach to in Germany, 19, 26, 129; hourly in United States, 17; inequality of, 13–14, 24, 55, 64; minimum, **67–71**, 76, 78–9, 151; *see also* earnings

Wages Councils, 67–8, 69

West Germany, 18, 26; *see also* Germany

White Paper proposal (1989), 113, 114
Windfall Tax, 88, 98, 128
work-sharing, 74–5
works councils, 111, 118

Youth Training Scheme, 39, 97

Warner Books now offers an exciting range of quality titles by both established and new authors. All of the books in this series are available from:

Little, Brown and Company (UK),
P.O. Box 11,
Falmouth,
Cornwall TR10 9EN.
Fax No: 01326 317444
Telephone No: 01326 317200
E-mail: books@barni.avel.co.uk

Payments can be made as follows: cheque, postal order (payable to Little, Brown and Company) or by credit cards, Visa/Access. Do not send cash or currency. UK customers and B.F.P.O. please allow £1.00 for postage and packing for the first book, plus 50p for the second book, plus 30p for each additional book up to a maximum charge of £3.00 (7 books plus).

Overseas customers including Ireland, please allow £2.00 for the first book plus £1.00 for the second book, plus 50p for each additional book.

NAME (Block Letters) ....

....

ADDRESS ....

....

....

☐ I enclose my remittance for ....
☐ I wish to pay by Access/Visa Card

Number ☐☐☐☐☐☐☐☐☐☐☐☐☐☐☐☐

Card Expiry Date ☐☐☐☐